ALLIED
DUNBAR
LIBRARY
MONEY GUIDES

MANAGING YOUR FINANCES

HELEN PRIDHAM

Second Edition

LONGMAN

© Allied Dunbar Financial Services Ltd 1990

ISBN 0–85121–6498

Published by

Longman Law, Tax and Finance
Longman Group UK Limited
21–27 Lamb's Conduit Street, London WC1N 3NJ

Associated Offices

Australia, Hong Kong, Malaysia, Singapore, USA

A CIP catalogue record for this book is available from the British Library.

Printed in Great Britain by Biddles Ltd, Guildford, Surrey.

Helen Pridham

Helen Pridham entered financial journalism after graduating in Economics from University College London. Formerly Assistant Editor of *Planned Savings* magazine, she is now a freelance journalist specialising in personal finance. She is the author of another Allied Dunbar Money Guide: *Tax and Finance for Women* and contributes regular articles to the *Daily Telegraph*, *Money Observer*, *The Glasgow Herald* and other publications.

Introduction

The choice of investment products gets wider and more confusing all the time. The Government has been trying to persuade us to invest more in shares through privatisations and personal equity plans. Building societies, banks and insurance companies are offering an ever increasing range of services, and each institution argues that its products are best.

Choosing the right financial product becomes much less difficult however, if you can sort out what goals you are trying to achieve and define your options for meeting them. Managing your finances efficiently means planning ahead.

Some people are put off financial planning because they feel it is only something for the very wealthy, or that it is too complex and therefore is best left to professionals. Both assumptions are wrong. Basic financial planning is within everybody's capabilities and the less money you have the more essential it is if you want to make the best use of your resources. You may want to move on to more advanced areas, where professional help is required but knowing your own needs will put you in a better position to judge the quality and suitability of the advice you are given.

Another objection to financial planning is that it is too time consuming. It is true you will have to invest some time especially at the beginning, but it is an investment that will pay a handsome reward.

Contents

7 Pension planning

8 Saving tax on your income and investments

1 Your aims

All of us have hopes, ambitions and expectations for the future. Some will be vague, some more specific. The more specific a goal is the easier it is to plan for. But for this reason, you may have allowed one goal, such as buying a better home or building up your business, to dominate and have ignored other goals completely.

The problem is that most of us tend to avoid sitting down and thinking out our aims clearly. Your excuse may be that predicting what is going to happen in the future is not possible.

This book will help you clarify your aims. Where you are unable to be precise, the answer is to use probability as your guide. For example, if you have young children you may foresee the possibility of sending them to private schools if you are unhappy with what the state provides. Taking a wait-and-see approach may make it extremely difficult for you to realise your intentions later. But by making plans which are flexible, you can be sure that you will have money available if you need it.

Indeed it is worth bearing in mind that even if your only desire is for your situation to remain as it is now, some planning is still necessary. A sudden accident, redundancy or a resurgence of inflation could throw you off course unless you make provisions to cover such situations. Consider some of the consequences of failing to plan, it could mean:

● Paying more tax than you need to

- Getting into financial difficulties if you suffer long term sickness
- Having to borrow heavily to finance the education of your children
- Losing money through having to cash in investments at the wrong time
- Having an inadequate income at retirement
- Leaving part of your wealth to the taxman instead of to your family

These and other problems can be avoided through financial planning.

What is financial planning?

Financial planning basically means finding the answers to four questions:

- Where am I now?
- Where do I want to be?
- What hazards lie in my way?
- Which is the best route for me?

The starting point for financial planning is a thorough appraisal of your current position. Don't be put off by this, although it is probably the most painful part of the whole exercise, it will have many positive effects which will make it well worth the effort. This book will guide you through it.

The important purpose that a review of your present situation will achieve is to help you spot ways in which you can make better use of your current resources. Many people are worth considerably more than they think but are not taking full advantage of what they have.

The next step is to work out your goals and to assess how far your current arrangements are getting you towards meeting them. It will then be possible to highlight potential problem areas. Many people think that they have made adequate plans for some things. But closer inspection reveals they are falling well short of their target.

Once this groundwork has been done the next step will be to decide what more you can do to achieve your goals. This will need to take account of time scale and risk.

Everybody needs to plan

In this book financial planning is treated as a two part process. Basic planning is essential for everybody. More advanced planning will be necessary for more specialist requirements.

Basic planning – Basic financial planning lays the necessary foundations for the successful management of your resources. It is often surprising when you get down to basics how the straightforward restructuring of current arrangements can make a big difference to your ability to plan for the future.

So basic planning encompasses such things as ensuring that you are getting the best credit deal and checking that you are repaying your mortgage in the most effective way. It involves making sure that your family is adequately protected against your death or illness. Making a will is part of basic planning to ensure that your possessions and wealth go to the people you intended. Once these fundamental questions have been sorted out then it is possible to look at ways of building up capital to meet your future requirements. Making provision for retirement will also form a part of everybody's basic planning.

Advanced planning – More advanced planning will be necessary if you have specific requirements. If you are a higher rate taxpayer, for example, saving tax will be a part of your planning. It is important not only to know how your income is taxed but also how tax affects various investments.

Certain areas of your life may require specific planning. If you have children, for example, you will need to make sure they are financially provided for whatever may happen to you. If you want to educate them privately you will have to plan for school fees. And if you want to ensure that they get the full benefit of your assets when you die you may have to carry out some inheritance tax planning.

If you have your own business, there are also special considerations to be taken into account. Not only will planning be necessary to ensure you get the best out of it now, and to guard against possible hiccups, but it will also be important to consider what will happen when you want to stop work.

How planning changes over time

Naturally financial planning requirements will change considerably over time as your circumstances change. Young people without children are likely to be primarily concerned with home ownership. A family with young dependent children will be particularly keen to protect their future welfare. When the children grow up there is more money available for investment and planning for retirement.

At retirement, your requirements change but the need for planning does not stop. In fact, it may become more imperative. You will not have another chance to build up your capital so planning to maintain its real value and thereby ensure long-term adequate retirement income is vital.

Certain other incidents may happen during your life that will make a change in your financial plans necessary. For example, if you cease being an employee and become self-employed, or

if your marriage breaks down and you find yourself divorced
and with a second family to plan for.

New legislation may also require planning adjustments to be
made. Tax changes in particular can make former plans
outdated and provide new opportunities for planning.

There is therefore a need to regularly reassess your financial
position and find out whether you are still on course for
achieving your objectives. Some people may feel that because
changes will occur this makes financial planning pointless.
In fact it makes it more important. Without financial planning
you are liable to be blown about like a ship in a storm.

Advice

Many people feel they need professional advice in order to be
able to plan their finances correctly. And indeed specialist
professional advice is often essential in some complex areas
such as inheritance tax planning. At the end of the book we
look at the various advisers and what services they offer.

But many people make the mistake of going to advisers
without knowing what they really want. This means that
they can end up being sold the wrong products.

You will be in a better position when you seek advice if you
already have a good grasp of your own finances and know
what you want to achieve.

The aim of financial planning

While we all have our own set of financial goals in life, it is
useful to remember that the main aim of financial planning

usually boils down to one thing – making sure we have sufficient income when we need it. This may be necessary to meet large bills, or for when we are sick or reach retirement. Helping you to find the best way of achieving that aim in its different forms is the objective of this book.

2 Your current position

How much are you really worth? What is the total current value of your investments? How much life assurance do you have? What will your pension be when you retire?

It is amazing how few people can answer such questions accurately. Most of us tend to jog along from day to day without giving too much thought to our overall financial position providing our income more or less matches our expenditure.

This makes choosing the right investment or financial product almost impossible. Although attractive terms or the promise of a high return may make one product seem a good buy, it could turn out to be completely inappropriate when all your circumstances are taken into account.

The first vital step in financial planning is therefore to draw up a comprehensive picture of your current financial position – a financial profile. This should be an eye-opening experience.

Even if you feel you have a good idea of how much you are worth – getting it down in black and white in front of you is a good way of concentrating the mind.

Your financial profile will serve two important purposes. It will provide you with a valuable basis for your future financial decision making and will give you an opportunity to review your existing arrangements.

Your financial profile

1 Your annual income

Note: You should enter gross income figures (ie before tax is deducted) and then deduct the total tax paid at the end

	You	**Your partner**
Earned income	....	....
Pensions		
state	....	....
private	....	....
Investment income		
bank interest	....	....
building society	....	....
share dividends	....	....
other	....	....
Other types of income (eg rent from property)	....	....

Fringe benefits (taxable values)

company car/petrol ....

medical insurance ....

other ....

Total gross income (before tax) £_____   _____

Tax paid on the above income ....

Total net income (after tax) £_____   _____

2 Your assets and investments

insert current values

Your home ....

Your holiday home ....

	You	Your partner
Cash on deposit		
bank accounts – current	....	....
deposit	....	....
building society accounts	....	....

National Savings ....

other ....

Investments:

gilts ....

shares ....

unit trusts ....

investment bonds ....

other ....

Possessions
car (not company car) ....

jewellery ....

valuable items in home (eg ....
collections)

total assets and investments (A)   £_____   £_____

Deposit and investment details
(For each type of account or investment, list relevant details, eg
names of building societies, name of account, rate of interest; National
Savings Certificate Issue, names of unit trust companies, name of
funds, etc.)

1 ....

2 ....

3 ....

4 ....

5 ....

6 ....

7 ....

8 ....

9 ....

10 ....

3 Your liabilities

	Amount outstanding	Repayment date	Interest rate	Monthly repayments
Mortgage type: *repayment/endowment/ pension*	....	....	....	....
Bank loans	....	....	....	....
Hire purchase	....	....	....	....
Credit cards	....	....	....	....
Store cards	....	....	....	....
Total liabilities (B)	£_____			Total monthly repayment £_____

4 Your net personal worth

Your assets and investments (brought forward from section 2(A)

You ....

Your partner ....

(A) Total £_____

(B) Total liabilities £_____

(C) Net personal worth (A–B) £_____

5 Your business

Business assets:

land ....

buildings ....

equipment ....

Total assets (D) ....

liabilities

amount outstanding	repayment date	interest rate
....	....	....
....	....	....
....	....	....

Total liabilities (E) ....

6 Your net business worth

(D) Total business assets   ....

(E) Total business liabilities   ....

(F) Net business worth (D–E)   £_____

Your annual income

If you are an employee noting down your annual earned income should be no problem. For the self-employed however, this can be more difficult because your earnings may well fluctuate from year to year. Taking the average of the last three years will probably give the best guide. Remember to take into account extra earnings from any additional freelance activities. Then make a note of your partner's earnings.

If you or your partner receive a pension, list this amount too. As well as a state pension, include any payments from company or private pension arrangements.

Make a note of any investment income you receive in the form of interest payments, dividends on shares etc. Even if you are not actually drawing your investment income but are allowing it to roll up, the taxman will still include it as part of your taxable income.

Investment income is often paid after deduction, ie net, of basic rate tax. However, it is important to establish the before-tax, ie the gross, amount because this is what the tax man adds to your other income to find out whether you must pay higher rate tax. This is normally a simple matter of adding back the 'tax credit' shown on your notification of interest or income to the net income you receive. From April 1991, the same will apply to bank and building society interest (unless you are a non-taxpayer and can receive it gross). In the meantime you will have to do a quick calculation in order to 'gross up' your interest. This can be done as follows:

Interest received $\times$ 100 $\div$ 75 = gross interest

So if for example you, receive £200 of net interest from your building society account the calculation would be:

£200 $\times$ 100 $\div$ 75 = £266.67

The above examples assume that tax has been deducted at the rate of 25%.

Besides your actual earnings you should also include the taxable value of any fringe benefits which you or your partner receive, such as a company car, petrol or medical insurance. If you are unsure of the taxable value, look at your most recent Notice of Coding (Form P2) from the taxman or ask your accounts department. Finally, deduct your tax payments in order to arrive at your net income.

Your current income is an important yardstick in your financial planning. As well as providing the money you need to live on and hopefully to save, it will determine the rate of tax you pay and will therefore influence your choice of investments. Those which may be advantageous for a basic rate taxpayer may not suit a high rate taxpayer. When you get to retirement you will have to consider the 'age allowance trap', more about this in Chapter 11.

Your income will also be a guide to the amount of life assurance and income protection you need, and how much provision you should make for a pension.

7   Your insurances

Life insurance

	Maturity date	Value at death	Expected value at maturity
Protection policy			
Life covered – you/partner/joint	....	....	....
Type of policy – term/whole life/endowment			
In trust – name beneficiaries:			
Mortgage policy			
Life covered – you/partner/joint	....	....	....
Type of policy – term/whole life/endowment			
In trust – name beneficiaries:			
Savings policy			
Life covered – you/partner/joint			
Type of policy – term/whole life/endowment			

In trust – name beneficiances: ....

Other policies

Life covered – you/partner/joint ....

Type of policy – term/whole life/endowment

In trust – name beneficiaries: ....

Permanent Health Insurance

you .... amount per annum ....

your partner .... amount per annum ....

Home Insurance

buildings cover ....

contents cover ....

Other insurance policies

....

8 Your pension plans

	you	your partner
Expected retirement age	....	....
Company schemes	*Expected pension p.a.*	*Expected pension p.a.*
current employer	....	....
previous employers	....	....
Personal pension		
type – with profits/unit linked/deposit	....	....
	Total £ ————	£ ————
Benefits on death lump sum	....	....
widow/widower's pension	....	....

Your assets and investments

Your home

Most people's greatest asset is their home. Despite the recent slowdown in house prices owning property has over many years proved to be a very good investment. So if you don't already own your own home, it is well worth planning for. If you are a homeowner, you need to keep its value in mind, so find out how much your property is worth by looking at the price at which neighbouring properties are selling. If not, ask an estate agent for an estimate of the market value. Don't ask for a formal valuation or you may be sent a bill.

Your home will enter into your financial planning in several ways. First, there is the need to ensure that it is adequately insured and that you are repaying your mortgage in the most efficient way. Secondly, it can provide security for further borrowing. Thirdly, if you want to pass your home on to your children, you will have to consider the impact of inheritance tax.

Cash and investments

Make a note of how much money you have that is readily available on deposit in your bank, building society or National Savings accounts, together with the current values of your longer term lump sum investments in gilts, unit trusts and shares.

You should also try to put a value on personal possessions of significant worth. Some may be items, such as antiques or a valuable collection of stamps, that could also be considered investments. Add up the total value of the items listed in Section 2 of your profile.

At the end of Section 2 give the details of your accounts and investments such as the names of building societies where you have accounts, the current rate of interest your money is earning, which issues of National Savings Certificates you hold, the name of the unit trust managers and type of fund if you are a unit trust investor, and the names of any shares.

Collecting all this information together will not only help you to work out how much you are currently worth, but it will also give you the opportunity to review the competitiveness of your existing investments. Points to look for will be discussed in Chapter 3.

Your liabilities

Having listed your assets and investments it is time to look at the other side of the coin — your liabilities. Most people's largest debt is their mortgage. But other debts can also mount up to considerable sums. Make a note in the table of any outstanding bank loans, credit card bills, etc., together with the rates of interest payable and the repayment dates where applicable. Also, note the monthly repayments to which you are already committed as these will reduce your income in Section 1. Financial planning is just as much about borrowing on the right terms as about investing and saving in the best way. Indeed with loan finance so readily available in recent years, many people have found themselves coming unstuck when they failed to keep control of their borrowing.

Your net worth

The moment of reckoning comes when you deduct the total of your liabilities from your assets and investments. If you are the owner or part owner of a business you will also have to take the final figure from Section 6 into account.

Your net worth will be particularly important in the context of inheritance tax planning and passing your money on to your children.

Your business

If you have your own business, this may well be your greatest investment and will be an important part of your financial planning. Make a note in the table of any business assets and liabilities.

Insurance

How does your existing insurance cover measure up? You may have your life assurance in several forms to provide your dependants with protection in the event of your early death, to repay your mortgage, or as an endowment savings plan. Make a note of how much cover you have under each category of policy and whether it is on your own life, your partner's life or a joint policy. Name also the type of policy if you know it – term, whole life, endowment. Note whether or not your life policies are written in trust.

Include details of other types of insurance policies that you have such as permanent health insurance (sick pay insurance) and home insurance.

Insurance is an area of your finances that you need to keep regularly under review in order to ensure that your cover is still sufficient and where appropriate, that you are still getting competitive terms.

Pension

What provision have you made for retirement, other than contributing to a state retirement pension? Have you thought about the age at which you wish to retire? If you want to stop working before state retirement age, you will need to make special provision. If you belong to a company pension scheme make a note of how much pension you are likely to receive when you retire. If you are not sure, your accounts or personnel department will be able to help. Don't forget about any pension you may have left behind when you switched jobs in the past. Make enquiries with former employers if you cannot remember the details.

If you are not a member of a company scheme or are self employed, you are responsible for your own pension provision. If you have taken out your own pension plans, list the estimated maturity values of these policies instead.

It is also important to be aware of the benefits your dependents will receive from your pension scheme if you die before retirement. Besides a dependant's pension, there may be provision under a company scheme for a lump sum benefit related to your salary.

Under a personal pension scheme, you may have had a choice if you took out a with profits plan of either a refund of premiums, premiums with interest or a refund of the full current value of the policy. Any additional life cover would have to be purchased separately.

With employees now able to decide whether to opt out of their employer's scheme and the state earnings related pension scheme being scaled down, pensions have become an even more vital part of everybody's financial planning.

An overview

Having completed your financial profile, you should now have a good overview of your current position. This will provide the foundation for your future planning.

If you want to be even more thorough you could document your current spending. This can be particularly useful if you find that too much of your money is slipping through your fingers each month without you knowing precisely where it is all going. But it requires considerable effort to do this accurately so don't worry if you feel like skipping this stage. To get a comprehensive picture you will have to map out your spending over a whole year, as some bills may only arise annually and others quarterly.

Fill in the annual budget chart (on pp 24 and 25) as best you can. Add your own spending categories. The more detailed your breakdown of spending is the more accurate it is likely to be. Last year's bills and receipts will be helpful although this year's bills will normally be higher so it is a good idea to include an allowance for inflation. Where you are not sure, make an estimate. Leave a second column to fill in your actual spending. If you want to be really precise you should keep a diary of your day to day spending for a month.

Unless you were already a very meticulous money manager, the process of completing your financial profile and documenting your current spending will probably have been a revealing exercise. In carrying it out, you may have spotted areas where improvement and further action is necessary. The next chapter which deals with your aims and assumptions should accentuate this process.

Your annual budget

	Jan	Feb	Mar	April	May	June	July	Aug	Sep	Oct	Nov	Dec
Balance from previous month	……	……	……	……	……	……	……	……	……	……	……	……
Income												
Salary (after tax)	……	……	……	……	……	……	……	……	……	……	……	……
Child Benefit	……	……	……	……	……	……	……	……	……	……	……	……
Pension	……	……	……	……	……	……	……	……	……	……	……	……
Other income	……	……	……	……	……	……	……	……	……	……	……	……
Total (1)												
Spending												
Housekeeping	……	……	……	……	……	……	……	……	……	……	……	……
Petrol	……	……	……	……	……	……	……	……	……	……	……	……
Meals at work	……	……	……	……	……	……	……	……	……	……	……	……
School meals	……	……	……	……	……	……	……	……	……	……	……	……
Entertainment and sports	……	……	……	……	……	……	……	……	……	……	……	……
Regular lump sums												
Mortgage	……	……	……	……	……	……	……	……	……	……	……	……
Credit repayment	……	……	……	……	……	……	……	……	……	……	……	……
Insurance	……	……	……	……	……	……	……	……	……	……	……	……
Life	……	……	……	……	……	……	……	……	……	……	……	……
House & Contents	……	……	……	……	……	……	……	……	……	……	……	……
Car	……	……	……	……	……	……	……	……	……	……	……	……

Rates								
Gas	......	......	......	......	......	......	......	......
Electricity	......	......	......	......	......	......	......	......
Telephone	......	......	......	......	......	......	......	......
Water	......	......	......	......	......	......	......	......
Car Tax	......	......	......	......	......	......	......	......
AA subscription	......	......	......	......	......	......	......	......
TV licence	......	......	......	......	......	......	......	......
Saving scheme	......	......	......	......	......	......	......	......
Irregular lump sums								
Holidays	......	......	......	......	......	......	......	......
Car Maintenance	......	......	......	......	......	......	......	......
Clothes	......	......	......	......	......	......	......	......
Repairs	......	......	......	......	......	......	......	......
DIY and garden	......	......	......	......	......	......	......	......
Christmas/Birthdays	......	......	......	......	......	......	......	......
Dentist	......	......	......	......	......	......	......	......
Other	......	......	......	......	......	......	......	......
Total (2)	......	......	......	......	......	......	......	......
Balance at month end (1–2)	......	......	......	......	......	......	......	......

3 Your future plans

Some obvious gaps in your financial provision may have emerged while you were compiling your financial profile, but you can only really start planning for the future once you have thought out your goals.

What are your financial aims? You may have some which are quite specific such as the desire to educate your children privately, to set up your own business, or to retire early. Clear aims such as these are the easiest to plan for. Most of us, however, tend to be rather vague about many of our goals. It is not usually because we don't have certain expectations for the future. It is more often because we have not been called upon to sit down and try to define them.

Being vague about your goals does not pay. At best it means your money is unlikely to be working as hard for you as it could, because you'll probably be keeping more in an easily accessible form, such as a building society, than you really need. At worst, you will end up a lot poorer – having to borrow money, having a lower income at retirement than you need, or even losing money on too speculative investments.

This is not to say that planning future goals is all that easy. Identifying very short term requirements may not be difficult, but after that it is often a matter of working with probabilities. Try and fill in the life plan chart as best you can.

A good starting point is to map out how old you and other members of your family will be at various points in the future, and what you are likely to be doing. For example, try to work

Life plan chart

Member of Family		5 years time	10 years time	15 years time	20 years time
you	age	....	....	....	....
	occupation	....	....	....	....
	expected retirement date		....		
your partner	age	....	....	....	....
	occupation	....	....	....	....
	expected retirement date		....		

Member of Family		5 years time	10 years time	15 years time	20 years time
child	age	....	....	....	....
	occupation	....	....	....	....
child	age	....	....	....	....
	occupation	....	....	....	....
child	age	....	....	....	....
	occupation	....	....	....	....
own parents	ages	....	....	....	....

occupations ....

partner's
parents   ages ....

occupations ....

....

Spending plans

major purchases   amount required   when/how/often

new car ....

other ....

....

Member of Family	5 years time	10 years time	15 years time	20 years time
property home improvement	....	....	....	....
move home	....	....	....	....
buy holiday home	....	....	....	....
children/grandchildren school fees	....	....	....	....
further education	....	....	....	....
pass on money	....	....	....	....
retirement pension	....	....	....	....

leisure
holiday ....

buy equipment for sport etc. ....

business
set up own business ....

other ....

General aims

Priority ranking 1 – 5

Provide for family   ....

Build up capital   ....

Improve performance of   ....
investments

Invest for extra income   ....

Reduce income tax   ....

Reduce inheritance tax   ....

Other   ....

....

---

out what jobs you or your partner are likely to be doing, whether you envisage a change of career or becoming self employed, or whether one of you may intend to spend time at home looking after children, and at what date you are both likely to retire. Think about your children's ages and whether they will be attending school or undertaking further education, and whether they will have left home or be married themselves. What about your parents and your partner's parents – have they already reached retirement, what state of health are they in? Is it possible that you may have to support one or more of your parents in their old age? Can you expect to inherit property when they die?

Once you have completed your life plan, it should help you considerably with the job of drawing up your likely future spending plans. For example, you can work out when and for how long you are likely to have to subsidise your children's education, when you will need money to start your own business or for your retirement income. Knowing how much you will need at some point in the future may not be easy but think how much you would need in today's money and try and make an allowance for inflation. (See the section later in this chapter on making an allowance for inflation.) The more you can put down in this table the better. Even if you feel doubtful about some of your plans, it will mean you have more options open to you if you have made some contingency provisions.

Besides having specific plans, you may also have a number of general aims, such as making sure your family is provided for, building up your capital and paying less income tax. You may feel that these have always formed an implicit part of your financial arrangements but once again making them explicit and prioritising them will help you to ensure that they really become part of your planning.

You should now have a better idea of the financial goals you are aiming at. But before looking at how these can be achieved in more detail it is a good idea to examine two possible obstacles which could inhibit your planning – one is your assumptions and the other your existing financial arrangements.

Are you making the right assumptions?

One of the reasons that many people fail to make adequate financial provisions is that they tend to make false assumptions such as:

- Long term sickness or accident – it won't happen to me!

Most of us dangerously underestimate the risk of illness. Statistics show that men are five times more likely to suffer an accident or illness which prevents them from working for more than six months than they are to die before age 65.

- If I am ill my employer will continue to pay my salary. It is true that around 9 out of 10 employees do receive some money from their employer's sick pay scheme, but only for a limited period. For one in three employees, it is for less than six months.
- The state will support me through a really long term illness. Do you know how much state sickness benefits are? Most people relying on state benefits alone would soon find themselves facing real financial hardship, and meeting major commitments such as mortgage payments or school fees could become impossible.
- If my partner dies I will be able to manage financially. If I cannot work I will claim state benefits. Once again state widows benefits are unlikely to be adequate for most families if the main breadwinner dies. Men should bear in mind that they will get no widower's benefit if their wife dies. If they have hefty mortgage payments and young children to look after they are likely to find it difficult to make ends meet without a salary coming in, or the extra burden of paying for childcare.
- Why should I worry so much about my retirement income? It will only be necessary for a short period. Many younger people fail to make sufficient provision for their retirement because they think they are not going to be around for long. But retirement can be a substantial part of your life. A man of 60 has an average life expectancy of 18.6 years and a woman 23.2 years.
- I have been contributing to a state pension all my working life. Why do I need a private pension as well? The current old age pension is less than half of average earnings. Not surprisingly therefore, many pensioners see their standard of living drop when they stop working.
- When I die everything I have will pass to my wife/husband anyway so I don't need to bother about making a will. This may be true if you only have very modest assets.

But if not your wife/husband may end up sharing her/his rightful inheritance with sundry other members of your family.

These may not have been your assumptions but you may have others. Don't leave it until it is too late to establish whether your assumptions are accurate.

Are your current provisions realistic?

Another trap which many of us fall into is that having made some financial provision, we tend to relax and assume that no further action is required. This can be particularly dangerous. First it assumes that the provision we made in the first place was sufficient and secondly that it will remain so despite possible changes in our own and external circumstances.

As we go through various aspects of financial planning we will be looking at ways in which you will be able to assess what provision is right for you which will enable you to compare the adequacy of your existing arrangements. But after that it will be up to you to review your circumstances regularly.

One of the greatest enemies of even the best laid plans is inflation. What may seem adequate now may turn out to be completely inadequate in the future because inflation has reduced its purchasing power. This can happen in a relatively short time. During the 1980's, for example, although inflation fell the purchasing power of the pound more than halved.

Inflation, therefore, cannot be ignored. As the future buying power table on page 37 shows, even if inflation is only 5% per annum your money will halve in value after only 14 years.

When you are planning for the future, it therefore makes sense to make a provision for inflation. If you think you will

---

Table 1

How the pound in your pocket shrank in value during the 1980s

Year	Value at start of year £	Annual Inflation %
1980	1.00	15.1
1981	0.85	12.0
1982	0.71	5.4
1983	0.67	5.3
1984	0.63	4.6
1985	0.60	5.7
1986	0.57	3.7
1987	0.55	3.7
1988	0.53	6.8
1989	0.49	7.7
1990	0.45	–

---

need £1,000 in today's money in, say 10 years time, and that inflation is likely to be around 5% over that period then you must actually aim to have £1,629 in money terms in order to have the same amount of purchasing power, as Table 2 shows.

Certain types of insurance policies, such as your home contents and buildings cover, may now be linked to an appropriate index to ensure that the cover remains sufficient. But there are still many areas where it is up to you to make sure that your financial provision keeps up with inflation, such as investing at least some of your savings in a way that they will maintain their real buying power – not just their monetary value.

Table 2
Future buying power of £1,000

Period	If yearly inflation rate over period is				
	3%	*5%*	*8%*	*10%*	*15%*
after 5 years	£863	£784	£680	£621	£497
after 10 years	744	614	463	386	247
after 15 years	642	481	315	239	123
after 20 years	554	377	215	149	61
after 25 years	478	295	146	92	30
after 30 years	412	231	99	57	15
after 35 years	355	181	68	36	8
after 40 years	307	142	46	22	4

How much you will need to maintain £1,000 of buying power

Period	If yearly inflation rate over period is				
	3%	*5%*	*8%*	*10%*	*15%*
after 5 years	£1159	£1276	£1469	£1611	£2011
after 10 years	1344	1629	2159	2594	4046
after 15 years	1558	2079	3172	4177	8137
after 20 years	1806	2653	4661	6728	16367
after 25 years	2094	3386	6848	10835	32919
after 30 years	2427	4322	10063	17449	66212
after 35 years	2814	5516	14785	28102	133176
after 40 years	3262	7040	21725	45259	267864

Approach to planning

In this book planning is dealt with in two stages. Although you may feel that there are some specific plans you would like to make, it is generally a bad idea to plan some parts of your finances and assume that the rest is fine. It pays to be systematic and work through your financial needs step by step. This way nothing is forgotten or neglected.

The first stage is to look at basic planning which everybody needs to do in order to ensure they have a sound financial framework on which to build. This means protecting and making the most of what you already have, making sure your family is provided for, looking at straightforward ways of saving and investing and providing for your retirement.

The second stage is to look at more advanced and specialist areas of planning, which may not be required by everybody, such as tax planning and business planning. There is also a chapter which deals with financial provisions for your children.

At retirement your financial needs will change. Ways of boosting retirement income are examined. And finally, Chapter 12 deals with how various advisers can help you.

4 Making the most of what you've got

The soundness of your current financial arrangements will have a decisive effect on your ability to plan for the future. If you are not making the most of your current income – for example, because you are paying too much for credit – it means you have less to set aside for future use. If you suddenly have to fork out a large sum to replace stolen items because you were underinsured, it could play havoc with your budget.

So your first step before getting down to future planning should be to run a health check on your current arrangements.

Is your home adequately insured?

Having worked hard to buy and furnish your home, it makes little sense to leave it unprotected. If you have a mortgage, your lender will normally insist that you have some house insurance in order to protect the security for its loan. But it is up to you to make sure you have enough cover.

If you don't you could end up having your claims 'averaged'. Many people assume this will only happen if they make a total claim but it will also apply to partial claims. So, for example, if your kitchen was gutted by fire and your insurer established that you had only insured your property for two thirds of its true value, then you would only get two thirds of the cost of putting your kitchen to rights. With fitted kitchens costing what they do today, this could leave you with a hefty bill to make up the difference.

Apart from providing the roof over your head, it is also worth remembering that your home is probably one of the largest investments you will ever make. Rising residential property values over the years have ensured home owners a good return on their money. It is an investment that you shouldn't take risks with.

Around one in ten policyholders claim on their house buildings policies each year. Weather and water damage are at the top of the claims list, then come fire and subsidence.

One of the most common confusions that arises when people are insuring their home is over the difference between the market value and the rebuilding cost of the property. One simple solution is to consider two identical properties, one overlooking a park and the other the council rubbish tip – the rebuilding cost will be the same but the market value definitely won't.

If you want to make your own estimate of the rebuilding cost of your property, send for a free copy of the Association of British Insurers leaflet called Buildings Insurance for Home Owners which lists average rebuilding costs per square foot for different types and ages of property in different parts of the country and gives detailed instructions on how to work out your sum to be insured. (It is obtainable by sending a stamped addressed envelope to ABI, Aldermary House, Queen Street, London EC4N 1TT).

Compare your final figure with your existing property cover and top up if necessary. Most insurers now index link their home buildings policies but don't forget that if you improve your home, such as by adding an extension, this will increase the rebuilding cost and you should review your cover.

Your Possessions

It is estimated that nearly one in four households in the country do not insure their home contents, and even among those that do over two out of three are under-insured.

The only way to be sure that your contents cover is sufficient is to go through each room in your house and work out the replacement cost of everything in it. Compare your final figure with your current level of cover. Is it enough?

If you don't want the hassle of totting up the value of your contents on a regular basis, a growing number of insurers are offering standardised levels of contents cover according to the size of your home. This means you avoid any danger of having your claims averaged, but does have the disadvantage that some householders could find themselves with either too much or too little total cover.

The cost of contents insurance has risen considerably in recent years mainly due to the increasing number of burglaries. In order to keep claims down and give householders an incentive to take extra precautions, many insurance companies are now offering premium discounts to those who install secure locks and burglar alarms. Older people who are at home for much of the day may also qualify for discounts. Another way of keeping your premiums down is to volunteer to pay part of each claim yourself.

Your bank account

The nature of bank accounts has changed considerably in recent years. Increasing competition from building societies has forced banks to give up making charges on accounts kept in credit and introduce interest earning accounts.

If you still have a traditional account it is well worth considering a change. Not only are you missing out on receiving interest when you are in credit, but because of the charges as well as the interest you must pay the bank if you go into the red, overdrawing is very expensive too.

Interest bearing accounts, however, vary considerably. Don't take too much notice of the interest paid. It is the charges that are most significant. Some accounts allow you to overdraw up to £100 without charge, levying a fixed fee plus interest if you exceed this amount. However, if you regularly overdraw by more than £100, you will be better off with an interest-only overdraft account. These are offered by several building societies.

Credit

Sensible use of credit has advantages. It can help you to budget and stretch your money further. But you must be careful to keep your lending within reasonable limits and make sure that you are borrowing on the best possible terms. This is often easier said than done. Offers of instant credit abound in every high street and come unsolicited through the post. Easy credit in recent years has led to increasing numbers of people borrowing more than they can afford and debt counselling services have had to be set up.

One suggested guideline for keeping yourself to a manageable level of borrowing is not to let repayments on loans other than your mortgage exceed 10% of your income. It is easier to keep control if you restrict yourself to one or two sources of credit. Try not to have more than one credit card or loan. In particular, you should always consider how you would repay your loans if you were hit by unemployment, sickness, death or a marital breakdown. Indeed if you are borrowing a large sum it is worth paying a little extra for insurance cover which provides for the repayment of the loan in case you are unable to work because of sickness or accident and sometimes redundancy too.

The problem for many of us when it comes to borrowing money is that we tend to go for the easiest option. But what is convenient is not always best. A far more important yardstick should be cost, although size of loan and length of repayment period will also influence your choice of the best type of credit. The relative cost of different types of credit over different timescales is indicated in Table 1.

In order to make cost comparisons you will need to find out the APR (annual percentage rate) of the loan or credit deal you are being offered. This takes the timescale of the loan into account and any extra charges such as commission or insurance. This way you can compare every deal on the same basis. But beware, although lenders are obliged to quote the APR, many will still quote you the flat rate of interest unless specifically asked, which can be considerably lower than the APR.

Table 1

The relative cost of credit

Short term credit *(A few weeks or so)*	*Medium term credit* *(One to five years)*	*Long term credit* *(Five years +)*
LIKELY TO BE CHEAP		
Free or interest-only authorised overdrafts Credit cards	Life policy loans Personal bank loans	Mortgage increase
LIKELY TO BE MOST EXPENSIVE		
Unauthorised over-drafts Store cards	Store & credit cards Hire Purchase	Finance company loans

Overdrafts

At the short-term end of the time scale, agreed overdrafts can be one of the cheapest and most flexible forms of credit there is. On some interest-bearing accounts there is even a free overdraft limit of £100 built into the account. Otherwise you will have to let your branch know beforehand. Check on possible fees and charges when you overdraw. If you regularly overdraw by more than £100, switch to a bank account that charges interest only. Avoid unauthorised overdrafts on which you will usually pay higher interest and higher charges.

Credit cards

In many people's eyes it is not money, but credit cards that are the root of all evil nowadays. However, used sensibly, credit cards are a relatively cheap and flexible means of spreading payments over a short period. If you time your purchases for the beginning of the account period – around the time you usually receive your bill – you can get up to eight weeks free credit if you repay your next bill in full. Spreading payments over a few months is not too costly either. You also get extra protection if you pay for something costing £100 or more by credit card, because the credit card company shares 'joint liability' with the supplier for making sure the goods or services are up to scratch. (This facility does not apply to charge cards.)

The choice of credit cards has increased considerably in recent years. They are now offered by both banks and building societies at different interest rates. Charity credit cards are also available where the company make a donation when a card is first issued and a small proportion of what you spend after that. Some credit card companies now charge an annual fee in exchange for a slightly lower interest rate and this is likely to become a growing trend. However, if you are someone who normally pays off their bill each month, such a card would not be advantageous. Watch out too for higher prices being charged for credit card purchases. If this becomes common practice and you only use your credit card as a convenient payment method, you will be better off paying at once.

If you do not regularly clear your credit card bill the danger is that you could find yourself running up a large bill that could take you a year or more to clear. That is when this type of credit becomes expensive. If you forsee this happening consider another type of credit facility, such as a bank loan. If it already has happened it still may be worth getting a bank loan to clear your outstanding balance. If you are moving home or renegotiating your mortgage, an even cheaper alternative may be to ask for a slightly higher mortgage in order to pay off your credit card debt.

Charge and gold cards, available if you are a high earner, do not offer extended credit — you have to pay off your bill each month. Their main advantage is that no spending limits are set and they have a very wide network of outlets which is useful if you travel abroad a lot. With gold cards, the generous overdraft facilities at favourable rates of interest are also useful.

Store cards

Store cards normally function like ordinary credit cards, but they are often more expensive. They do sometimes offer special perks such as shopping evenings and discounts. But the disadvantage is that they may discourage you from shopping around in other stores to find the best price for the goods you want. Best avoided unless you clear your bill every month.

Personal loans

For major purchases such as a new car, new furniture or to meet other substantial outlays, ask your bank if you can have an ordinary loan. If this type of loan is not available, personal loans are often the best way of spreading the cost. If you get your loan in advance, you may also be able to negotiate extra discounts from the retailer on the same basis as a cash buyer.

Banks typically offer personal loans for amounts of between £500 and £5000 for terms of between six months and five years. The interest rate is normally fixed until the end of the repayment term, so you know precisely what your payments will be. This will work in your favour if interest rates generally rise during the term, but is not so attractive if they fall. Find out if there are any penalties for paying off your loan early.

Besides banks, many building societies are nowadays offering personal loans. These are worth enquiring about. You may be charged a preferential rate as an existing borrower

Hire purchase

The cost of hire purchase varies considerably according to the type of goods you are buying. When you are buying a car the rates can be competitive, although you may lose out by not being able to negotiate a cash sale discount. But for other consumer goods, hire purchase is normally an expensive option.

Insurance policy loans

If you are strapped for cash you may consider surrendering your insurance policies early. This is normally unwise, however, as with most insurance policies surrender values in the early years could well be less than the contributions you have made. An alternative to surrendering is to borrow against the value of your policy.

Interest rates on policy loans are competitive and can be less than for personal loans or overdrafts. The loan is repaid

from the payout when your policy reaches the end of its
normal term and you may even be able to roll up the interest
and pay it off in the same way.

However, if your policy is being used to pay off your mortgage
a policy loan may not be available.

It is also usually possible to borrow alongside the value of a
self-employed or executive pension plan if you have one.
Some security is normally required such as your home or
shares. The loan is normally repaid from the tax free lump
sum you can take at retirement, so think carefully before
taking this type of loan because it means you will have less
money available at pension age when you will often need it
most.

Mortgages and remortgages

It is widely acknowledged that buying your own home is one
of the best financial decisions you can make, and there are
plenty of institutions around these days that are ready and
willing to lend you the money you need. Providing you
borrow from a reputable building society, bank or insurance
company, mortgages are also one of the cheapest forms of
borrowing available.

Rising house prices in recent years have also made it possible
for many people to raise extra cash by unlocking the equity
in their property (ie the difference between your existing
mortgage and the current value of your home). There are
several different ways in which this can be done. The best
solution is normally to increase your mortgage with your
existing lender. Another is to remortgage your property by
taking a larger loan from another institution to pay off your
original loan and give you the extra finance you require. Less
satisfactory is a second mortgage or secured loan. Steer clear
of finance companies for remortgages or second mortgages.
Their rates tend to be higher and they are likely to charge
a redemption fee if you repay your loan early. Always keep

an eye on your mortgage rate, especially if you are with a less well-known lender. If your interest rate gets too high, it may be worth switching. But if you have a joint mortgage with someone you're not married to, taken out before August 1988 on which you are getting extra tax relief, remember you may loose the extra relief if you change lenders.

Repaying your mortgage

If you are about to take out or increase a mortgage, or even if not, it is a good idea to reconsider the method you are using to repay your mortgage. Mortgage repayments account for a substantial chunk of most people's monthly outgoings so it is important to be sure that you are using the best possible route.

There are various aspects of the different mortgage repayment methods to consider. One side is the monthly cost but the flexibility and potential benefits of each method also need to be taken into account. You may find it worthwhile paying more for extra benefits.

There are four main ways of repaying a mortgage: a straight forward repayment mortgage, an endowment mortgage, a pension related mortgage and a Personal Equity Plan (PEP) mortgage. Their main differences are summed up in Table 2.

The relative monthly cost of each method is shown in Table 3. A low start endowment is the cheapest option to start with, but after time becomes the most expensive. Which is the cheapest of the other three options depends on the mortgage rate. At higher interest rates a repayment mortgage is the cheapest in terms of monthly cost. The second least expensive is the PEP mortgage.

The attraction of endowment and pension mortgages is that the cost is offset by the possible cash surplus after you have

Table 2

Methods of mortgage repayment

Type	Repayment	Endowment	Pension	PEP
Monthly repayment	Interest + Capital (+ MPP premium*)	Interest + Endowment Premium	Interest + Pension contrib. + term assurance	Interest + PEP contribution into unit trust + term assurance.
At end of term	Mortgage repaid	Mortgage repaid + possible cash surplus	Mortgage repaid + pension for life	Gains permitting, mortgage paid off in instalments during term.
Advantages	Flexibility to extend term, convert to interest only etc in case of cash difficulties	Provides possible cash surplus at end of term, enables maximum tax relief on interest to be claimed	Tax relief available on pension contribs and interest, provides pension at end of term	Income + gains on PEP tax free, possibility of repaying mortgage before end of term if growth sufficient, resulting in cost savings.
Disadvantages	No cash surplus at end of term	Lack of flexibility, especially on with profits endowments.	Less money for retirement	Risk of share price fluctuations.

*Mortgage Protection Policies will pay off your mortgage in case of your early death. They are not obligatory but are strongly recommended.

Table 3

Mortgage cost comparisons

The monthly cost for a couple, where the man is 35 and the woman is 32, repaying a £60,000 mortgage over 25 years assuming both are basic rate taxpayers.

Mortgage type	Initial net monthly cost at differing mortgage interest rates:			
	8%	10%	12%	15%
	£	£	£	£
Repayment*	437	507	582	699
Low start endowment**	403–456	491–544	578–631	709–762
Endowment	444	531	619	750
Personal Pension***	415	503	590	721
Personal Equity Plan*	422	510	597	729

* Includes premium for joint life mortgage protection policy
** Endowment premiums increase for first five years, table shows premiums in year one and year five.
*** Personal pension plan taken for the man only to age 60, includes premiums for two single life term policies on the man and the woman

repaid your mortgage, while with a pension related mortgage you also get a pension for life. Although there is no guarantee with either of these methods that the cash sum provided will be sufficient to repay the mortgage, the likelihood of a shortfall is remote. Nevertheless, the size of the payout will vary considerably according to the investment performance of the insurance company. So check out a company's past results before taking out a policy.

If you are unable to afford both a mortgage and a pension plan, a pension related mortgage is a good idea. But remember that you will be sacrificing part of your retirement benefits to repay your mortgage. Therefore if at future date you find you can afford to do both, it would be better to pay for your mortgage separately so that you can preserve the maximum amount of your pension for your retirement.

PEP mortgages have only been available since 1989. Regular payments are made into a unit trust PEP, on which all investment income and capital gains are tax free. The aim is that as the gains build up within the PEP they are used to pay off parts of the mortgage leading to considerable savings in interest payments. However, PEP mortgages are regarded as more risky than other types because of likely fluctuations in share prices. A PEP mortgage is therefore probably not suitable for a first time buyer.

Summing up

- Check how much house insurance and home contents you should have. Compare with current level of cover. Top up if necessary.
- Take a look at your methods of borrowing:
    - avoid store cards and hire purchase, they tend to be expensive forms of credit
    - if your outstanding credit card balance gets too large, consider using a cheaper form of

borrowing to clear the balance, such as a bank loan

- for larger amounts it may be worth extending your mortgage.

- Keep an eye on your mortgage rate, if your lender is charging more than average a switch could pay
- Check your method of mortgage repayment – would you benefit from a change

5 Meeting your basic aims

For most of us our most valuable asset is our family and our primary aim is to make sure they are happy and secure. It is surprising, however, how often we fail to make them top priority in our financial planning. We may be working hard to support them from day-to-day but fail to make adequate provision for them in case disaster strikes.

The trouble is that none of us like to think about our own death or sickness. But just stop and consider for a moment how your family would manage if you became seriously ill or died in the coming year. Would they have enough to cope with all the expenses of running a home, let alone be able to afford a decent holiday?

The first of your basic financial aims should therefore be to ensure that, whatever happens to you, your family does not suffer undue financial hardship.

Just as important is to make sure that when you die your wealth goes to the people you want to get it. Don't assume this will happen anyway. You need to make a will. Later on in this chapter we look at who gets what if you don't make a will.

How much protection do you need?

Before considering the different types of life insurance available and how you can protect yourself against long term sickness, it is important to decide how much cover you really need.

Various yardsticks for the right amount of life insurance have been suggested such as providing a lump sum of ten times your annual income. But your requirements may clearly change at different times of your life. A young couple without children will not need too much life insurance. But if they are relying on two incomes to make ends meet, they should make sure they have enough cover to pay off their debts, such as the mortgage, so that if one partner dies the remaining partner does not have to struggle on alone meeting the repayments.

For families with dependent children the need for cover is greatest. And the best way of working out how much is simply for each partner to sit down and calculate how much income they would need if they had to manage on their own. Fill in the life insurance calculator on page 56. Your partner should fill in the column headed 'You' giving the amounts he or she would need if you died and you should do the same in reverse. Even if one of you is not currently working because there are young children to be cared for, you should consider the extra income you would need to pay someone else to look after the children. Certain expenditure may no longer be necessary. If your mortgage is already covered by a life policy, for example, the outstanding loan will automatically be repaid and so monthly repayments will cease. In other areas, it may be necessary to spend more, for example if you have a company car your partner may need to find the money to replace it and pay the running costs.

When you have worked out the income that would be needed, it is easier to calculate how much life insurance cover you require. But first of all, check back to your financial profile to see whether you or your partner will receive a pension from each other's pension scheme. If so this can be deducted from the income figure you need.

The next step is to find out the lump sum required to provide the desired level of income. Such a calculation cannot be

absolutely precise, of course, since much will depend on the
level of interest rates at the time the money is invested. The
only solution is to allow as much leeway as you can in your
reckoning. After all, no widow or widower is likely to
complain if they are left too much income to manage on. The
other factor to take into account is that what may seem to
be a realistic sum now could have been whittled down by
inflation by the time it is paid out. The best way round this
problem is to choose an insurance policy that offers an
indexation facility giving you the guaranteed right to increase
your life cover in line with inflation. As a guide the table
shows the amounts you would need to invest to provide
various levels of income at different interest rates.

Table 1

Lump sums required for various levels of income according to interest rates available

*Annual income required**	*Interest rate available*			
	7%	10%	12%	15%
	£	£	£	£
£3,000	42,860	30,000	25,000	20,000
£5,000	71,430	50,000	41,670	33,332
£7,000	100,000	70,000	78,350	46,667
£10,000	147,860	100,000	83,350	66,667
£12,000	171,430	120,000	100,000	80,000
£15,000	214,290	150,000	125,000	100,000

*No allowance made for income tax made or inflation

Another reason for being generous in your calculations is that
while the payout from a life insurance policy will be free of
tax, the income it produces once it is invested will be taxed
in the normal way. Once again it is therefore difficult to
make exact provision because the amount of your partner's
tax liability will depend on how much other income he or
she receives and what tax rates are at the time.

When you have worked out the amount of cover you need,
look back to your financial profile and compare it to your

existing life insurance, not counting those policies covering outstanding debts such as your mortgage. This will reveal the amount of cover you are short of. Try to repeat this exercise each year to make sure your insurance cover remains in line with your requirements and has not been eroded by inflation.

Your life insurance calculator		
	You	*Your partner*
Income your family would need on your death (excluding repayments of debts covered by existing insurance eg mortgage)	_____	_____
Less pension	_____	_____
Income required from life insurance	_____	_____
Likely lump sum required to provide this income (use Table 1 as guide)	_____	_____
Less existing insurance cover (not including cover for outstanding debts, such as mortgage)	_____	_____
Insurance cover required	_____	_____

When your children leave home, the need for the protection type of life cover will normally diminish but you may still need life insurance for other reasons, for example, in connection with business, or to cover inheritance tax liabilities. These uses will be discussed in Chapters 9 and 10.

Types of life insurance

Unless you are in the fortunate and unusual position of not requring further life insurance, your next decision will be to consider the type of policy you are going to need.

Term assurance

If cost considerations are paramount, there is little doubt that term assurance is your best bet. This is the cheapest form of life cover available because it pays out only if you die within the insured period, say 5, 10 or 25 years. There is no investment element so you get nothing back if you survive the term. It can be used to provide either a lump sum or a regular income. It is also a good way of providing for loans to be repaid in case of early death. For example, if you don't have an endowment mortgage, a term policy can be used to cover your outstanding loan.

If you choose term assurance make sure you get a renewable and convertible policy that enables you to take out a further policy or to switch to an endowment or whole life policy at a later date, without further evidence of health. This means you will not be left without any life cover at the end of the term if your health deteriorates.

Term assurance can be purchased even more cheaply in

Table 2				
Approximate monthly cost of £100,000 initial cover under convertible term assurance				
	10 year term		*15 year term*	
Male age next birthday	30	55	30	55
Monthly cost	£18	£125	£20	£170

conjunction with a personal pension contract. Like your pension contributions, the premiums will qualify for tax relief at your highest rate of income tax.

Whole life insurance

The drawback of term assurance is that unless you renew or convert to another policy, your life cover runs out at the end of the insured period. And if you do take out another policy you will have to pay higher premium rates to take account of the fact that you are older. What many people also dislike about term policies is the idea of paying into a contract from which they get no cash return if they survive.

The answer to these problems is to take out a whole life insurance policy which gives you permanent cover regardless of changes in your state of health and at premiums which remain related to the age at which you started your policy. In the past traditional whole life policies were rather an expensive option but the introduction of unit linked whole life policies has brought the cost down. These policies offer high levels of life cover at modest cost, plus the possibility of a growing cash-in value depending on the performance of the underlying investment fund. The cost is kept down by assuming a realistic growth rate when premiums are calculated. Policies are reviewed after ten years and then at five year intervals in order to check that growth has been at the expected level. If it has been greater than expected your life cover will be increased, if it has been lower you may be asked to top up your premiums.

The great advantage of most unit-linked whole life plans is their flexibility. Normally you are allowed to adjust your life cover within certain limits to suit your circumstances. For example, you can take the maximum life cover when your children are small, reduce it when they leave home and perhaps increase it again later to cover possible inheritance tax liabilities. Cover can also normally be increased in line with inflation.

One point to bear in mind, however, is that although unit linked whole life policies can build up a cash value, they should never be regarded as a savings contract. They are first and foremost designed for protection and your savings can be more productively invested elsewhere.

Table 3

Typical benefits payable per £25 monthly premium on flexible unit-linked whole life policies, where life cover is guaranteed for first 10 years

Age	Sustainable sum assured* £	Est. cash value after 10 years £	Maximum sum assured £	Est. cash value after 10 years £
30	55,000	2,300	135,000	1,500
50	15,000	1,750	27,000	750

*Sustainable throughout life of policyholder providing assumed unit growth is at least 7.5 per cent

---

Endowment policies

Endowment policies provide some life assurance protection but they are primarily designed for savings purposes in the context of which they will be discussed in the next chapter.

The cost of life cover

Apart from the type of insurance policy you choose, the amount you pay for life cover will also be influenced by a number of factors including: your age, your sex, medical history, your current health, whether you smoke, the amount of insurance you want and your occupation and hobbies. The younger you are the lower your premiums will be, while women (who have a longer life expectancy than men) are normally charged the same premiums as men four years younger than themselves.

If you want a high level of life insurance, or have suffered illness in the past your doctor may be asked for a medical report or you may be asked to undergo a medical examination. Single men may also be required to have a blood test to ensure they are not HIV positive. But even if you are in poor health, you may still be able to get life cover at a somewhat higher premium.

Putting life cover in trust

Whichever form of life cover you opt for it is a good idea to put it in trust for your partner and dependants under a suitable trust form. The best trusts are ones which allow you the flexibility to meet changes in your personal circumstances, eg on divorce or on the birth of children. Writing a policy in trust will ensure that the benefits are paid out immediately after your death, otherwise there may be a delay until probate is granted. It also enables the death benefits to pass to your children without falling within your estate and being liable to inheritance tax. Most life offices will be able to provide you with the trust forms for use with their policies.

Insuring against sickness and disability

Most of us recognise the need for life insurance. But very few of us make any provision against sickness or disability. Yet statistics show that men are five times more likely to suffer an accident or illness that stops them working for six months or more than they are to die before the age of 65.

Advances in medical science mean that more people are surviving illnesses and accidents that would have previously resulted in death, but they are not necessarily in a fit state to return to their former jobs. There are currently over one million people claiming state invalidity benefit which means they have been off sick for six months or more.

If you do fall sick you may be lucky and get sick pay from your employer for several months but after that you will have to rely on state sickness benefits which are unlikely to be adequate to enable you to maintain your standard of living.

The best way to protect yourself and your family from financial hardship in the event of ill health is by taking out income protection insurance. In insurance jargon this is known as permanent health insurance (PHI) because once you take out a policy the insurers can't cancel it whatever your state of health may be.

Under a PHI policy you can decide the amount of income you want in the event of sickness, but there is normally a limit of 75% of your earned income less state benefits. (The insurers don't want you to be better off sick than at work!)

Although it is possible to choose a level income, it makes more sense to opt for benefits that increase by a fixed percentage or in line with a suitable index both before and during payment to ensure they maintain their real value. Bear in mind that if you are subject to long term disablement you could be drawing benefits for many years.

Apart from the amount of benefit, other factors that will influence how much you must pay for PHI include – your age, your sex, your health, your occupation, and how quickly you want the benefits to start.

There are some disabilities that insurers will not pay out for, commonly injuries caused by war or civil commotion, self inflicted injury or abuse of alcohol or drugs. For women, restrictions are normally placed on pregnancy related conditions – some insurers exclude them altogether, others will cover them if they continue for 13 or 26 weeks after the end of the pregnancy. Also excluded may be injuries that occur during certain types of sports.

Another point to watch is the company's definition of disability. Most will pay out if you cannot follow your own occupation, but some will only do so if you are unable to follow 'any remunerative occupation' which is much more restrictive.

PHI cover lasts until normal retirement age. Traditionally policies have been on a non-profit basis so unless you fall ill you get nothing back. However, in recent years a growing number of unit linked insurers have started offering policies where a cash value accrues if investment growth within the policy has been better than expectations. But this is mainly only of interest if you cash in early, as towards the end of the term larger deductions are made to cover the increased risk of ill health so the cash value decreases.

Table 4

Permanent Health Insurance – Typical annual premiums required to provide £100 week benefit payable to age 60

	Deferred period 4 weeks £	Deferred period 26 weeks £
Man aged 29	120	55
Woman aged 29	170	77
Man aged 39	170	80
Woman aged 39	240	115
Man aged 49	260	130
Woman aged 49	380	190

*Premiums applicable to those in Class 1 occupations, ie office and professional workers.

If you are able to buy PHI cover under a company scheme it will usually pay you to do so as premiums tend to be lower. But if you are buying a policy individually, don't let price be your only guide. With this type of insurance it is particularly important to ensure that the terms and conditions suit your requirements, and that the company has a good record of meeting claims. It may be wise to seek the help of a financial adviser when taking out this type of cover.

Hospital cash plans/personal accident and sickness policies

Some policies appear to offer similar cover to PHI but at much lower cost. However, there are some vital differences.

Hospital cash plans, as their name suggests, pay you a cash sum while you are in hospital and sometimes while you are convalescing. But before taking one of these plans bear in mind that the probability that you will go into hospital in any one year is relatively low – there is around a 1 in 13 chance. And even if you are admitted, the average stay in hospital is less than ten days.

Personal accident and sickness policies pay out cash sums if you are unable to work because of accident or sickness but the period of payment is normally restricted to two years. Thus if you suffered long term disablement you would soon find yourself without any income.

Critical illness cover

Another type of cover worth considering, however, is a critical illness policy which will pay out a lump sum if you are diagnosed as suffering from a serious condition, such as cancer or a heart attack. Such an illness can cause a considerable change in your lifestyle and there could be many ways in which a lump sum would be useful, eg to make modifications to your home, seek further medical advice or pay off debts. If you don't suffer one of the illnesses specified in the policy the lump sum will be paid out on your death like an ordinary life insurance policy. But this type of policy is no substitute for a PHI policy which will provide financial support if you suffer from almost any type of accident or illness.

What if you die without making a will?

Two out of three people do not make a will. The reason is that they normally assume that their husband or wife will automatically inherit everything when they die anyway. But this is not necessarily the case.

There are fixed rules about who gets what if you die intestate – without a will – which may not coincide with what you intended. Here is a broad guide to the provisions, in some cases their operation can be quite complex.

If your possessions are worth under £75,000 then everything will go to your widow, or widower. But for larger amounts the position is more complicated. The first £75,000 will go to the remaining spouse, plus personal effects such as furniture and a car. The remainder will be divided into two halves. One half will go to your children if you have any, while your widow or widower will get a life interest in the other half, that is he or she would receive the income from it – interest on deposits, dividends on shares etc. When that partner dies, the half in which he or she had a life interest will pass automatically to the children.

If there are no children, the widow or widower will get

everything up to £125,000 and half of the rest. The other half would go to the parents of the spouse who had died.

Where there are children, but no surviving husband or wife then the whole estate is divided among the children equally.

The assets of an unmarried person, without children, go in the first instance to his or her parents and if they are dead to the person's brothers and sisters or their children. Under the rules of intestacy, none of the property of a divorced person goes to their ex-spouse.

If you own a property jointly with someone else, whether you are married or not, you are assumed to be 'joint tenants' and full ownership passes automatically to the surviving partner if one of you dies. If you have opted to be 'tenants in common', the dead person's share in the house passes to his or her estate and will be dealt with according to the rules of intestacy unless a will has been made.

Under the rules of intestacy restrictions also apply to the investment of money held in trust for young children, a situation which could arise if both parents were, for example, killed together in an accident.

Even if you feel that the intestacy rules are acceptable bear in mind is that the rules of intestacy change occasionally and it is the rules in force at your death which will apply. In Northern Ireland the rules are slightly different and in Scotland there is a complex system of 'prior rights' which govern what happens to your property on death.

By making a will you can eliminate uncertainty and ensure that the right people inherit your money. You can make specific bequests for different parts of your property.

It is, of course, possible to make a do-it-yourself will if your affairs are straightforward. But to avoid misinterpretation and other potential problems arising after your death it will probably pay in the long run to ask a solicitor to draw up

your will for you, especially if you want to do something
unusual like disinheriting somebody, or if you have
substantial assets like a business. If you have assets overseas,
such as a holiday home in Spain, seeking professional advice
is particularly essential. If you don't already have a solicitor,
ask your friends and colleagues or ask the Law Society for
a list of those in your area.

When you draw up a will you will also have to name executors
to carry out your wishes. Choosing a member of your family,
subject to their agreement of course, has the advantage that
their services come free but using a bank or a solicitor or
accountant means you get their expertise. A compromise is
to choose one of each type.

Once you have made a will remember to review it regularly.
If you need to make changes don't just amend the original.
You will need to add an extra part, a codicil, or draw up a
fresh will.

Finally, make sure you leave your will in a safe place, such
as your bank, and inform your relatives where you have left
it.

Whether or not you draw up a will, however, a claim can be
made against your estate by anyone who you were wholly or
partly maintaining prior to your death under the provisions
of the Inheritance (Provision for Family and Dependants)
Act 1975.

Summing up

- Check whether your existing life insurance policies would
  provide enough income for your family if you died early
  and top up if necessary
- Consider how you and your family would manage if you

were seriously injured in an accident or suffered long
term illness. Take out income protection insurance.
* Make a will. If you have one already, check regularly that
it still reflects your wishes.

6 Accumulating and investing capital

There are so many savings and investment schemes available these days that it is not surprising that many people end up with their money in a hotchpotch of schemes, with their choice often mainly determined by the advertisements that caught their eye when they had spare cash available. Alternatively, they despair of finding the right schemes and have all their money in a building society.

If you are going to manage your finances effectively the first thing to remember, whatever your investment objective, is that your first aim must be to protect what savings and capital you have. This does not necessarily mean putting it all into a bank or building society, where the monetary value is maintained but where it is likely to lose its purchasing power over time. It means investing as much capital as you can where you have the best prospect of preserving its purchasing power. This is different from taking every opportunity to increase the real value of your capital, which often means taking more risk. Any attempt to do this should only involve a small proportion of your capital at any one time.

So what is the best way of protecting your capital? Unfortunately there is rarely one perfect answer (except when you view the situation with hindsight). The solution is to avoid extremes and aim for a balanced portfolio.

Achieving a balance involves a number of factors:

- It means investing for both the long term and the short term. Although you need some capital for a rainy day where you can get at it in a hurry, don't keep all your

money on short term deposit in a bank or building
society, because you are unlikely to need it all at a
moment's notice. But don't, on the other hand, have
everything tied up in long term investments because you
never know when you may need some of it.

- It means getting a spread of risk. Try not to put all your
  money into one type of investment. Economic trends
  change and so do investment attitudes. Having different
  kinds of investment – fixed interest deposits as well as
  shares, overseas as well as UK holdings – means you can
  benefit in some way whatever the investment trend.
- It means not relying on one investment manager or
  company for all your needs. Some may be good in some
  areas and some in others. No one company has yet
  cornered the market in investment expertise.

The chart below indicates the three main elements which most
people should have in their investment portfolio:

Elements of an investment portfolio

A	B	C
Bank/Building Society Deposits National Savings	Gilts	Share Related Investments

The degree of spread you have in your portfolio will depend
partly on how much money you have and partly on your
attitude to risk. If you only have a small amount put by, then
fixed interest investment of the types which fall into
categories A and B could form all or most of your portfolio.
The size of element B relative to C will be determined by
how cautious you are.

The actual investment products you choose in each category
will be influenced by whether your objective is to build up
capital or generate income. In this chapter the main emphasis

is on building up capital. Chapter 11 on retirement planning looks at ways of investing for income.

Another factor which needs to be taken into account is tax. There are several tax free investment schemes available nowadays which can play a valuable role in helping you maximise the returns on your portfolio. But you shouldn't let their tax advantages outweigh basic investment considerations.

More about risk

Some types of investments are certainly more risky than others and it is as well to bear in mind the old investment adage – the higher the return, the higher the risk. So don't be seduced by advertisements which promise large percentage returns without being aware that you are taking a gamble.

But it is also important to consider that timescale can have a major influence on risk.

The risk of a short term investment direct in shares or through unit or investment trusts was well demonstrated by the 1987 stock market crash. Share prices moved up strongly during that year until October when the market fell back sharply wiping out nearly all the gains that had been made. It showed how you can make large profits within a very short time, but it also showed how you can make a large loss if the stock market takes a nose dive. Over the longer term, however, historical trends show that with a portfolio of shares you are likely to achieve significant capital growth and your shares have a good chance of maintaining their value against inflation or even outpacing it. A long term investment in shares is therefore less risky. Table 1 shows that despite short term dips the long term trend in share prices and share income has been upwards.

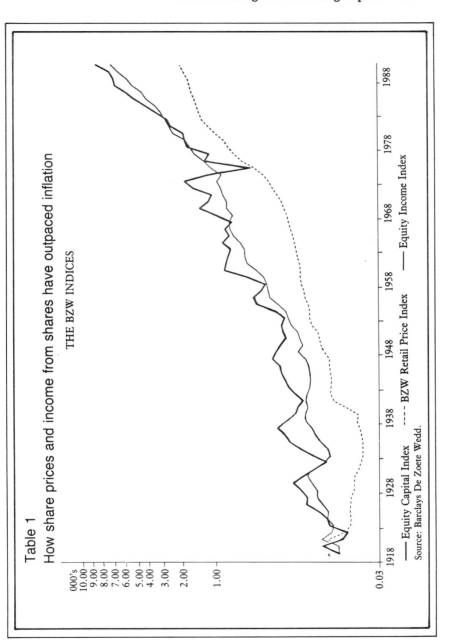

Table 1

How share prices and income from shares have outpaced inflation

THE BZW INDICES

—— Equity Capital Index   ---- BZW Retail Price Index   —— Equity Income Index

Source: Barclays De Zoete Wedd.

Table 2

Average net rates of building society interest over the last 15 years

Source: *Building Societies Association*

Table 3

Investment Comparisons
(Results of different forms of saving and investing over different periods to 1.1.90)

	1 year £	5 years £	10 years £
Lump Sum £1,000			
Bank account	1,045	1,310	1,870
Building society account	1,086	1,516	2,298
National Savings Certificates	1,075	1,528	2,274
Gilts*	1,048	1,436	2,649
Average UK General unit trust	1,201	2,199	6,765
Personal Equity Plan**	1,210	2,301	7,444
Retail Price Index	1,058	1,291	1,949
Regular Savings £30 per month			
Bank account	369	2,461	5,248
Building society account	375	2,256	5,637
Gilts*	367	2,101	5,617
Wih profits policy***	–	–	8,525
Average UK General unit trust	366	2,516	10,152
Personal Equity Plan**	369	2,582	10,579
Retail Price Index	368	2,062	4,794

*As measured by FTA British Government Allstocks Index
**Hypothetical result of PEP invested in average UK General unit trust
***Result of a Norwich Union policy

Source: Planned Savings Data Services

With a building society account, on the other hand, short term security is good. The monetary value of your capital will be maintained and you can be sure of getting some interest. Over the long term, though, you have no way of knowing whether interest rates will go up or down and you risk the real value of your capital being seriously depleted by inflation. Table 2 showing the movement of the building society investment rates over the last 15 years indicates just how unpredictable your returns from a building society investment can be.

The chart in Table 3 shows how returns on different types of savings and investment plans compare over the short, medium and long term and how they have matched up to inflation as measured by the Retail Price Index.

To be absolutely sure of matching inflation you can invest in the Government's index linked gilts and National Savings Certificates where the value of your money is maintained in line with the Retail Price Index. And it therefore makes sense to include them as part of your portfolio. However, once again, to put too much emphasis on them would be unwise because it would mean that in times of low inflation you would miss out on better rates of return elsewhere.

Your emergency fund

Your first step in planning your investments should be to make sure you have an emergency or reserve fund from which you can obtain cash at short notice to meet unexpected bills. This saves you from losing money by possibly having to cash in longer term investments early.

How much you keep in your reserve fund should be related to your outgoings and commitments. One suggested guideline is that you should have an amount equal to between three and six months normal outgoings. Try to maintain this fund at your chosen level, topping it up again if withdrawals are made.

Table 4

Risk and timescale – your main choice of investments

	Short term *0–3 years*	*Medium term* *3–10 years*	*Long term* *10 years plus*
Low risk	Building society bank and National Savings deposits.	National Savings, gilts, building society SAYE, TESSAs.	Index linked gilts, tax exempt friendly society plans.
Medium risk		PEPs, unit trusts, investment trusts, investment bonds	PEPs, endowments, unit trusts, investment trusts, investment bonds, blue chip shares.
High risk	All share-related investments, alternative investments, commodities.	Shares, Business Expansion Scheme, alternative investment, commodities.	USM, OTC shares, alternative investments, commodities.

Low risk investments

Banks

Bank deposit accounts can be a useful low-risk investment for the short term or a home for your reserve fund. But check that you can't get a better interest rate from a building society.

In recent years, the banks have put some effort into attracting people with lump sums of £1000–£2000 into higher interest accounts, some with cheque book facilities. These accounts pay variable rates of interest but it is possible for larger depositors to put money into term accounts which pay a fixed rate of interest for a period of say six months or a year.

Building societies

Building societies now offer a much wider range of services and products than previously. But for small investors, those with shorter time horizons, and as the first part of an investment portfolio, the traditional savings and deposit accounts are still most appropriate. The attraction of building society accounts for non-taxpayers will also increase from April 1991 because interest will be obtainable without tax deducted.

The basic building society account is the ordinary share account which gives completely free access to your money. But it also pays the lowest rate of interest. Nowadays, it is possible to earn extra interest on lump sums of as little as £100 or £200, with instant access providing you keep the required minimum in your account. Higher interest rates are also available if you are prepared to give notice of say 30 or 90 days of withdrawals, with an interest rate penalty if you make a withdrawal without giving notice.

Changes in rates and conditions on building society accounts nowadays are frequent. So you need to keep a regular check on what is available and whether your own society is giving you the benefit of its latest improvement.

TESSAs

If you are able to lock some of your savings away for five years in a bank or building society account you would be well advised to do so through the new Tax-Exempt Special Savings Accounts (TESSAs) which become available on 1 January

1991. The schemes were announced in the 1990 Budget in an effort to encourage increased saving. Providing you leave your savings untouched for the full five years all interest earned will be tax-free.

You will have the choice of making regular savings of up to £150 per month, or making lump sum deposits. The maximum lump sum deposit will be £3,000 in year one and £1,800 per year in the following years up to a total of £9,000 altogether.

Any individual over 18 will be able to open a TESSA. Husbands and wives may have one each.

It is important to note, however, that after five years the account will cease to be tax-exempt so any further interest will be taxable in the normal way. A new account can be opened at that time, though, so £3,000 of your accumulated savings could be transferred across.

Although early withdrawals of capital from a TESSA will lead to a loss of tax advantages, you will be able to withdraw up to the full amount of interest credited to the account less basic-rate tax. The balance of the interest will have to stay in the account until the end of the five-year period.

The exact details of how TESSAs will work, such as the rate of interest payable, whether it will be fixed or variable and whether there will be penalties on early withdrawal, are being left to the financial institutions so it will be necessary to shop around for the best deal.

An existing, but often neglected tax free savings scheme is the building society Save As You Earn scheme. This is a uniform savings plan operated by a number of building societies whereby you save a fixed amount of up to £20 per month for up to five years when you are paid a bonus of 14 months' payments tax free. If you leave the money for another two years the bonus is doubled. The return over five years is 8.3% or 8.6% over seven years. You can withdraw your money early but a lower rate of interest is paid.

National Savings

National Savings offers a range of products that are often useful for both short and medium term investment and for different types of taxpayers.

Until April 1991 when composite rate tax on building society and bank accounts is abolished, the National Savings Investment Account will still be the most appropriate home for deposits for non-taxpayers because interest is paid without tax deducted.

For medium-term investment there is the Capital Bond which pays a guaranteed rate of interest over five years, without tax deducted. But if you are a taxpayer tax is payable annually on the interest even though you don't receive it until the end of the five-year period. For this reason National Savings Certificates are likely to be more attractive to taxpayers since the return they provide, which is also fixed over five years, is completely tax free.

With the resurgence of inflation Index Linked Savings Certificates are looking attractive again. They pay a guaranteed bonus on top of index linking free of tax. For the maximum bonus, the certificates must be held for five years.

For monthly savers, there is the National Savings Yearly Plan which requires fixed monthly payments for one year. To qualify for maximum interest you must leave your money untouched for a further four years. Interest is fixed for the full five year term whenever a new plan is taken out and is tax free.

Those who are really keen to save tax should also note the concession on the National Savings Ordinary Account which entitles you to the first £70 of annual interest tax free, the entitlement is doubled on a joint account.

Table 5: Low risk choice

	Minimum Investment £	Interest	Tax position	Withdrawal notice
Banks				
Deposit account	1	v	Interest paid net of composite rate tax*	7 days
Fixed term accounts	2,500	f	As above	After agreed term.
High interest account	2,000	v	As above	None
Building societies				
Ordinary share	1	v	Interest paid net of composite rate tax*	None
Instant access	200	v	As above	None
Notice account	500	v	As above	30 – 90 days
National Savings				
Ordinary account	1	f	First £70 tax free, further interest paid gross but taxable	1 – 7 days
Investment account	5	v	Interest paid gross but taxable	1 month
Savings certificates	25	f	Tax free	18 days
Index linked certificates	25	l	Tax free	18 days
Capital bond	100	f	Interest paid gross but taxable	3 months
Yearly plan	20 pm	f	Tax free	14 days
Gilts	None	f	Interest can be paid gross but taxable, gains tax free	
Index linked gilts	None	l	As above	
Friendly Society Tax Exempt Plans	13.50 pm	v	Tax free	Should be held for full term of 10 yrs

Interest: f – fixed, v – variable, l – linked to RPI

*From April 1991, interest is paid net of basic rate tax but can be paid gross to non-taxpayers

Gilts

One of the main ways in which the Government borrows money from the public and institutions is through the sale of Gilt Edged Securities. They pay a fixed rate of interest, known as the 'coupon', and if held to maturity or 'redemption' you get back a guaranteed amount of capital.

With Index Linked Gilts the value of the income increases in line with inflation, and the capital value too but you can only be sure of benefitting from the latter if you hold the stock until it matures.

Capital gains on gilts are free of tax. In order to get maximum capital gains you need to buy low coupon stock. You can sell your stocks prior to redemption on the stock market but the price you get will depend on the state of the market and will fluctuate.

High coupon gilts are useful if you want a guaranteed regular income. More details on this aspect and how to buy gilts are given in Chapter 11.

Tax exempt friendly society plans

Friendly societies played a prominent part in Victorian times as self help organisations. After fading from prominence, they were rediscovered in the late 1970s and early 1980s because of their ability to offer tax free savings plans.

However, the amount that can be saved in these plans is limited. Premiums are restricted to £13.50 per month or £150 per year. Although societies no longer have to invest half your money in gilts or other risk-free investments, many still offer this type of investment option which should be chosen if you prefer a low-risk investment. It makes them a useful halfway house between TESSAs and PEPs which invest only in shares. One disadvantage of the plans is that they must be held for a full ten-year term, otherwise returns are limited to the premiums paid.

Medium risk

Unit trusts

As a short term investment, any investment in shares must be regarded as high risk. Over the medium term, direct investment in shares remains high risk though the risks can be lessened if you have a sufficiently diversified portfolio – that is your investment is spread over a large enough number of shares so that if one or two go wrong the effect will be diluted. But this is only possible if you have a large capital sum.

Smaller investors can achieve a spread of risk, however, by investing in pooled funds such as unit trusts. These provide ready made portfolios of perhaps 50 to 100 shares. They do not take all the risk out of investing in shares, since if the stock market as a whole falls so will your stake, but they do reduce the risk substantially.

Other advantages of investing in unit trusts rather than direct in shares are that you don't have to worry about when to buy and sell individual holdings – professional investment managers do it for you. The costs of unit trusts are also relatively modest compared to direct investment. You normally pay 6% when you first invest and an annual management fee of 1–2% thereafter. The actual price of the units will depend on the value of the underlying investments.

One problem which faces investors, however, is choosing from the wide variety of unit trusts available. In recent years funds have become increasingly specialist – investing in particular types of stocks or individual countries.

The snag is that the more specialist the fund, the less the risk is diversified and the more volatile its performance tends to be. In order to minimise risk it is much better to start off with good broadly based UK growth or income unit trusts and then add on some general overseas funds. With these types of funds the investment manager is not too restricted as to the stocks or the countries he can invest in and can take advantage of the best opportunities available.

Once you have a good base of broadly spread funds, you could consider putting a small amount of your money into more specialist funds. But beware of buying after a period of strong growth because there is a danger that you will be investing at or near the peak of that market. If that is the case, it could mean the market is about to go into a period of decline and your money will go along with it.

It is easy to switch between unit trusts as investment conditions change and recently some unit trust groups have started offering cash funds which can be used if markets are unstable.

Besides choosing the type of fund you will also have to decide on a unit trust group. It is a good idea to examine the overall performance record of different groups. Don't just look at short term results. Check for long term consistency. Refer to specialist publications such as *Planned Savings*, and *Money Management* and *Money Observer* which publish unit trust performance statistics every month.

As well as accepting lump sum investment, many unit trust groups also run monthly savings plans. These schemes have much to recommend them. You are not committed to saving for any particular period and you can cash in when you like, or alternatively, once you have built up the required minimum investment you can stop saving and leave your money invested until you need it. Another advantage of saving plans is that you do not have to worry so much about getting the timing of your investment right because you will be buying units at all stages of the market cycle. Because you buy more when prices are low it keeps the average price of your units down. This is known as 'pound cost averaging'.

Income on unit trusts is paid net of basic rate tax. Capital gains tax is payable but can usually be avoided because of each investor's annual CGT exemption. However, the best way of investing either a lump sum or regular savings in unit trusts is through a Personal Equity Plan (PEP). (For more detail see below and Chapter 8.) In a PEP all your investment gains and investment income on your unit trusts will be tax free.

However, if you have a large sum to invest it is worthwhile considering the unit trust portfolio management services which some groups offer. They will compile a portfolio of their own unit trusts, and in some cases other groups funds also, and will switch your money around between the funds as market conditions change. You will normally be charged extra for this service.

Investment trusts

Investment trusts and unit trusts have some similarities. For example, both offer managed portfolios of shares. But there are some important differences. Investment trusts are companies in their own right. The price of the shares is therefore determined, like the shares of other companies quoted on the Stock Exchange, by supply and demand. For this reason the price of shares does not always match the actual value of the trusts investments. In recent years many investment trusts have been selling at a discount which means you could in effect buy shares through them at a reduced price, but receive dividends based on the full value of the shares. The discount only becomes a disadvantage if it is larger when you want to sell your investment trust than when you bought it, but in general discounts have tended to narrow over the past few years and this has given a useful boost to their performance.

Investment trust shares can be bought at low cost through the managers. Lump sum and regular savings schemes are available. Some managers also offer PEPs.

Full performance listings for investment trusts can be obtained from the Association of Investment Trust Companies or from the specialist magazine, *Investment Trusts*.

Investment bonds

Investment bonds are issued by insurance companies. They offer a choice of funds investing in UK and overseas shares, property, fixed interest and cash deposits, as well as managed funds which hold a mix of these investment elements.

The main difference between unit trusts and investment bonds is in their tax treatment which can work either in favour or against the investor. Higher rate taxpayers can gain from bonds because the investment income is taxed as that of the life company at a maximum rate of 25% and rolls up within the bond until encashment. On unit trusts, the investor must pay his normal rate of tax on any income.

On encashment of a bond, higher rate tax may be payable. But first any gain will be top-sliced which may help to reduce the tax bill. Top-slicing involves the gain, ie the difference between the bond's current value and its original purchase price, being divided by the number of years the bond has been held and the resulting 'slice' added to the bondholder's income in the year of encashment. The tax rate payable on that slice will determine the tax rate applicable to the whole gain. Thus higher rate tax may be avoided altogether if encashment takes place when the investor is paying a lower rate of tax, such as after retirement.

Capital gains are also treated differently with a bond. Unlike a unit trust where the capital gains tax liability rests with the individual on disposal of the units, with a bond the insurance company must make a deduction for capital gains tax, though this is normally less than the full rate which in any case is not more than 25%. For investors with substantial capital gains already, bonds can therefore be advantageous. But if your gains are less than the annual exemption you could be better off with unit trusts.

One often stated advantage of investment bonds is that it is possible to switch between investment funds either free of charge or at a considerably lower cost than between unit trusts. Switching funds close to retirement into a fixed-interest fund can be a useful way of consolidating gains. But, in general, it is worth bearing in mind that whatever investment vehicle is used it is not easy to get timing of switches right and you could lose more than you gain.

Investment bonds can be useful if you are investing for income because it is possible to make withdrawals without incurring an immediate tax liability. This aspect is dealt with in Chapter 11.

Personal Equity Plans

Personal Equity Plans (PEPs) were introduced by the Government in 1987 as a means of encouraging wider share ownership. Their great attraction is that you can invest up to £6,000 per year in shares and receive all investment income and capital gains from them free of tax. If you want to invest in shares, unit or investment trusts always do so through a PEP first. But don't let the tax advantages make you forget the risks of investing in shares. (For more details about how PEPs work see Chapter 8.)

Endowments

With profits endowments

Conventional with profits endowment policies are a traditional means of long-term saving. You pay a regular monthly or annual premium for a minimum of ten years and many people use longer-term policies for mortgage repayment. These policies provide a modest amount of life insurance. But the bulk of your premiums are invested by the insurance company in a mixture of property, shares and fixed interest securities. The profits it makes on these investments are distributed to policyholders in the form of bonuses.

There are two types of bonuses. First, there are annual bonuses which once added to your policy cannot be taken away. Insurance companies aim to keep these fairly stable in order to smooth out fluctuations in the investment markets and provide steady growth. In the good years some investment gains are held back to maintain bonuses when market conditions are not so good. At the end of the term, or on your earlier death, a final bonus is added that is aimed to give you the benefit of rises in capital values during the period of your policy. These bonuses are more likely to fluctuate from year to year in line with investment markets. The payout you receive from an endowment is free of tax in your hands provided you hold it for at least ten years, or three quarters of its term, if less.

Although it is possible to cash in a with profits endowment early, you will normally lose money if you do. In the early years of the contract you may not even get back as much as you have paid in premiums, and after that you will often lose the benefit of the final bonus if you surrender early.

Before you buy a with profits endowment policy, always check the company's past performance record over a reasonable period of time, not just the past year. Although there is no guarantee that its future results will be similar, it is the best guide available.

Unit linked endowments

Unlike with profits endowments where there is normally a steady build up in bonuses funded by retained profits, the growth of a unit linked policy will always depend on the value of the underlying investments. This means you get the full benefit of any gains, but you are not cushioned if the investment market falls. You can, however, make your own choice of investment fund, and many people prefer to minimise their risk by opting for a managed fund which invests in a spread of equity, property and fixed interest holdings.

One of the advantages of unit linked endowments over with profits endowments is that surrender penalties often cease before the end of the term so you can cash in somewhat earlier and still get the full value of your savings.

For many investors, however, the charging structure on unit linked endowments makes them poor value compared with unit trust savings plans. But they may be worth considering if you are a high rate taxpayer because, as with investment bonds,

Table 6

Medium risk choice

	Minimum Investment	*Tax Position*
Unit Trusts	£25 p.m. or £500 lump sum	Interest paid net of basic tax, gains subject to CGT
Investment Trusts	£20 p.m. (practical min. lump sum £500–£1,000)	As above
Investment Bonds	£1,000	Tax paid on the fund by insurance company, higher rate taxpayer may be liable to further tax on cashing in.
Personal Equity Plans	£20 p.m. or £1,000 lump sum	Tax free
Endowments	£10 p.m.	Tax paid by insurance company, payout tax free to investor

the investment income and capital gains within the policy are treated as the insurance company's and taxed at a maximum rate of 25%. Moreover, the payout from the policy will be tax free provided it's a qualifying policy and is not cashed in for ten years or three quarters of its term if less than ten years.

High risk

Shares

Direct investment in shares has become increasingly popular in recent years mainly thanks the Government's privatisations of companies, such as British Telecom, British Gas and the water authorities, in which shares were offered to the public at prices which virtually guaranteed a quick profit.

However, the steep fall in the Stock Market in October 1987 has made clear that in the short term it is just as easy to lose money on shares as it is to make profits.

Besides timescale, the degree of risk involved in share investment will also be influenced by the type of shares you hold. The safest type of shares are those of large well established companies with good track records – the so-called blue chip companies, or alpha stocks. They are unlikely to show spectacular growth or to pay very high dividends, but they tend to show steady progress and you are not likely to lose your shirt. At the other end of the risk scale are penny shares, the shares of small and recently formed companies that are traded on the Unlisted Security Market (USM) and the Over The Counter Market (OTC). These are shares from which you may be able to get high dividends and enormous profits if you are able to pick a winner, but the risk of the companies going bust and you losing all your money is considerable.

In some instances a small direct holding in a share may be advantageous because of the perks that are offered to shareholders such as discounts on the company's products or services.

The cost of buying and selling shares varies. Stockbrokers are free to set their own commission so it pays to shop around. Some banks and building societies offer their own share-dealing services. But most banks will merely channel your request to a stockbroker and may make a handling charge for doing so. A telephone share-dealing service is also available.

If you want to deal direct with a stockbroker ask your friends and colleagues for recommendations or write to the Stock Exchange and ask for names of brokers in your area prepared to take on new private clients.

Many brokers are happy to provide a dealing only service for small investors, but they are less likely to be prepared to advise you on which shares to buy or to manage a share portfolio on your behalf unless you have at least £30,000–£50,000 to invest.

Even more risky than shares themselves are options which give you the right to buy or sell shares for a given price within a fixed period. Unless you have a gambling instinct it is best to steer clear of this market.

Business Expansion Scheme

Through a Business Expansion Scheme you can invest in the shares of new and growing companies which want to raise extra cash, and enjoy tax relief on your investment. A popular, lower risk type of BES scheme is that which invests in property to rent. But investing in new companies always involves some risk and you also need to bear in mind that your money will be tied up for at least five years. (More about BES in Chapter 8.)

Alternative investments and commodities

You can, of course, invest in all sorts of things besides
financial assets, such as wine, stamps, antiques, works of art
and commodities – gold, silver, coffee, cocoa, etc. But all of
these items are high risk investments. They do not produce
any income and the potential gains are often determined by
unpredictable factors, such as fashion or weather. However,
if you get enjoyment anyway out of things such as good wine
or fine antiques you may feel that the risks are worth taking
regardless of what happens to the price.

Gold coins are a popular form of commodity investment but
the gold price is also very unpredicable.

Summing up

- Make sure you have an emergency fund for immediate
  cash needs.
- Bear in mind the need to protect the purchasing power
  of your capital as well as its monetary value.
- Aim for a balanced investment portfolio with a spread of
  risk.
- Bear in mind the tax position of your investments and
  consider switching to tax free schemes.
- Compare long term performance when selecting
  investment managers.

7 Pension planning

More attention is focused on pensions nowadays than perhaps
at any other time in the past. In 1988, the Government made
some important changes affecting both state and private
pensions. Its aim was to encourage people to take more
responsibility for their pension and give them more freedom
to do so.

It is never too early to start planning your pension if you want
to ensure that you are going to have a comfortable
retirement.

The price for leaving your retirement planning too late or not
bothering to plan at all can be high. It may mean not just
sacrificing the luxuries of life, like an annual holiday but
having difficulty meeting the cost of basic necessaties, like
heating.

The problem with pension planning is that for most of our
working lives we tend to have other priorities such as bringing
up a family or building up our careers or businesses. At the
same time, many people find it difficult to imagine that they
will one day be pensioners for a significant part of their
lifetime.

However, as the following table of average life expectancies
at different ages shows, a man retiring at age 60 has a life
expectancy of nearly 19 years. A woman in the same position
can expect to live 23 years.

Note that these are only average figures which means that
though half the men aged 60 will not survive to age 80 the

Life expectancy		
Age	Men Yrs	Women Yrs
55	22.0	27.6
60	18.6	23.2
65	15.1	19.1
70	11.9	15.3
75	9.2	11.8
80	6.9	8.9
85	5.0	6.4

other half will survive even longer. If you tell a man aged 60 that he has a one in three chance of being alive at age 85, he may start to look at his financial planning in a rather different way.

Another factor is that more people are retiring early. This means an even longer period to plan for and a shorter period in which to plan.

Saving for retirement

In order to ensure that you have an adequate income in retirement, you have to be prepared to give up some of your income while you are working.

Using a pension plan to save for retirement has clear advantages over any other form of savings. Successive Governments have, in the past, encouraged private pensions through tax incentives and look like continuing to do so in the foreseeable future.

These tax incentives are:

- Contributions to a pension scheme qualify for tax relief

- Pension funds pay no UK taxes, so they can build up faster than taxed investments
- Pension benefits can be taken in a tax efficient way, in part as a tax free lump sum.

What makes up your pension?

The first step in pension planning is to get an idea of exactly what you can expect from your existing pension arrangements. Your pension can come from up to three sources.

The state

There are three types of state pension which are paid from state retirement age, which is 65 for men and 60 for women.

The basic old age pension

To qualify for a full basic old age pension you must have paid (or been credited with) National Insurance Contributions for approximately 90% of your working life. If you haven't done so, then you'll get a reduced pension but you must have a contribution record of at least a quarter of your working life to qualify for any pension at all. (Credited contributions are given to those who are out of work and are claiming unemployment benefit or income support, or who have home responsibilities and are claiming child benefit or attendance allowance. Men over the age of 60 who are no longer working automatically qualify for credits.)

Married women who have paid the married woman's reduced NI contribution do not qualify for a pension in their own right. However, when a husband reaches age 65, he will receive an extra pension for his wife based on his own contributions. But this will not be as much as an extra single person's pension. If you are a married woman still paying the NI contribution, you would be well advised to switch to full contributions unless you are within a couple of years of retirement or due to stop working for another reason.

One important point for the self-employed is that the basic old age pension is the only pension that they qualify for from the state.

The Graduated Pension

This is a small pension which is given to those who paid graduated National Insurance Contributions between 1961 and 1975.

State Earnings Related Pension Scheme (SERPS)

This is a pension scheme which came into force in April 1978. It was originally designed to ensure that everybody retiring from April 1979 onwards would receive a pension equal to 1.25% of their qualifying earnings for each year of employment from April 1978 onwards, up to a maximum of 20 years. This would give a pension of 25% of earnings based on the average of 20 years earnings (and for people retiring from April 1999 onwards it would be based on the best 20 years). A widow's pension is also provided. However, changes have now been made to these benefits which will affect those retiring after the end of the century.

SERPS benefits are to be scaled down between the year 2000 and 2010 so that anyone retiring after that date will receive a pension of only 20% of qualifying earnings instead of 25%. Moreover, instead of being calculated on your last 20 years earnings, SERPS will be based on your lifetime average qualifying earnings. Widow's pensions will also be reduced.

It is now no longer compulsory for an employee not in an equivalent company pension scheme to be a member of SERPS. The pros and cons of opting out of SERPS are discussed later in ths chapter.

If you want to know how much state pension you can expect at retirement, you can apply for a forecast on form BR19 available from DSS offices.

Your company

If you are employed by a company, then you may belong to an occupational pension scheme. Most schemes are known as 'final salary schemes' because your pension at retirement will be calculated as a certain proportion of your final salary for each year that you have worked for the company. In most final salary schemes, you will get 1/60th of pay for each year of service (a less good scheme will give you 1/80th) which means that you have to work at least 40 years with the company to get the maximum pension of two thirds of your final salary.

The other type of pension schemes are known as 'money purchase' schemes. These rely on all contributions (both from yourself and your employer) being invested in a fund which builds up through capital growth and reinvested income. At retirement, your pension will depend not on your final salary (except for calculating the maximum amount permitted) but on what the value of your share in the fund has grown to by the time you retire. Consequently much depends on the skill of the investment managers.

Money purchase schemes tend to be favoured by small employers who are nervous of the open-ended financial commitment of a final salary scheme.

What is important, regardless of what scheme you belong to, is to get as good an idea as you can of what your pension will be worth when you retire (and don't forget to base it on today's money so that you can relate it to your current salary). However, don't assume that the terms and conditions of your scheme will always be the same as they are today. It is best to ask your own pension department exactly what your pensionable service will be at retirement and what kind of income you can expect.

You should also check out how generous your employer is to retired employees and what allowances are made for inflation. Are pensions increased regularly and by how much? Is an increase guaranteed? Even if increases are not guaranteed, your company may have a good record of discretionary increases which will mean that you can be confident that you are in a worthwhile scheme.

How much you will be paying for your pension will vary from scheme to scheme. The luckiest employees are those in non-contributory schemes where the employer foots the bill in total, but these are comparatively rare. Normally, your employer will contribute around 10% and you will be required to pay around 4% to 5% of your earnings.

It can no longer be compulsory for employees to be members of a company pension scheme.

Your own pension plan

If you are self employed, or employed by a company which does not have a pension scheme, then you may have made your own pension arrangements. If you took out a pension plan prior to 1 July 1988, you will have what is known as a 'Section 226' scheme or a 'Retirement Annuity Contract'. Anybody with such a plan can continue to contribute to it until they reach retirement. Nowadays anyone taking out a new plan is sold a personal pension plan.

The main differences between the two types of pension plans are that under a Section 226 policy you can take up to around one third of your pension fund as a tax free cash sum, whereas under personal pension plans it is limited to 25%. In addition, under a Section 226 policy the earliest you can take your pension benefits is age 60, while a new style Personal Pension allows you to retire from 50 onwards. It is possible to switch from a Section 226 policy to a new style Personal Pension Policy at any time, but you cannot make a switch in the other direction.

What both types of plans have in common is that your benefits will be determined by the amount you invest and the investment performance that has been achieved ie, they are money purchase plans. In order to get a guide to what your future pension is likely to be you should ask your insurance company for a projection.

Planning your pension

Once you have established your existing pension provision, you can look at ways of improving it where necessary. If you are relying solely on the state pension scheme you should consider topping up your benefits by taking out a personal pension plan. You should also consider whether you would get a better deal by opting out of SERPS. If you have already opted out, you should check whether it is time to opt back in.

If you are a member of a company pension scheme you could make extra savings through AVCs. If you are moving jobs you will need to think about whether it is a good idea to join your new employer's scheme. These matters are looked at in more detail below.

Personal pension plans

All employees not in company pension schemes and the self employed can take out personal pension plans into which they can save between 17.5% and 40% of their earnings up to a maximum of £64,800 (this figure is revised each year in line with the RPI) and get full income tax relief on their contributions. The limits vary according to age. Contributions are invested in pension funds that are free of all UK income and capital gains tax. These tax advantages mean that personal pensions are an excellent way to save for an extra pension at retirement.

Under a personal pension plan, you can start to draw your pension at any time between the ages of 50 and 75. Infact you do not actually have to retire before starting to draw your pension. You can take up to 25% of your pension fund as a tax free lump sum, although this will mean a lower regular pension. The pension will be paid for life and will be taxed as earned income.

To ensure your contributions are maintained on your behalf if you are unable to work as a result of illness or injury, you should make use of a 'waiver of premium' option. You can also take out life assurance protection alongside your pension plan and qualify for tax relief on your premiums.

Withdrawing from the State Earnings Related Pension Scheme

Unless you have already opted out you will definitely belong to SERPS if your company does not have its own pension scheme, and even if it does you may still be a member of SERPS. If you are unsure ask your wages department.

Since 1988 it has been possible for employees to withdraw from SERPS and take out a personal pension plan instead and the Government is encouraging this by allowing the DSS to pay that part of your National Insurance Contributions which was previously intended for SERPS into your own pension plan. In addition, they will pay an additional bonus to anyone opting out before 1993 as a special inducement to persuade you to leave SERPS.

Your employer may also contribute to your personal pension plan but that's a matter for negotiation between you and your employer.

The benefits built up by the DSS contributions will be called 'Protected Rights Benefits'. The main difference between those benefits and the benefits you build up by your own contributions is that no part of the DSS contribution benefits can be taken as a cash lump sum. It must all be taken as a lifetime pension and may not be taken any earlier than state retirement age. This is why it is a good idea to make extra contributions so you have more flexibility as to how you take those benefits.

The decision whether to withdraw from SERPS is not an easy one. The main reason for you to do so is if there is a good chance that a personal pension will produce a higher return for you than a state pension. By and large, it does not make a great deal of sense for older people (ie men of around 50 or over, and women of around 40 or more) because the amount paid by the DSS into a personal pension plan will not provide better benefits than those provided by SERPS. For younger ages, it could make more sense but this decision will need to be reviewed at regular intervals. If you do decide to opt out of SERPS now, it might make sense to move back into the scheme at some point in the future – though this is a decision on which you will need competent advice. Ask a financial adviser or pension provider for comparative illustrations so you can decide when you should opt back into SERPS.

Withdrawing from your company pension scheme

If you wish to withdraw from your employer's own occupational pension scheme you can take out a personal pension instead. Once again, this is likely to be advantageous to younger people particularly those who anticipate moving jobs several times before they settle down in a long-term career. However, is a decision that should not be taken at all lightly – your occupational scheme may provide you with a number of extra benefits such as life insurance and sick pay insurance that will be more costly for you to replace on an individual basis.

One reason why some people may want to leave their company pension scheme is that they do not believe the benefits they will get will be particularly high and that they will get better results from investing in their own personal pension scheme. However, you should do your sums very carefully indeed. Don't forget that although you may feel that your pension benefits look small, they are being paid for at least in part by your employer. If you take out a personal pension plan, there's no guarantee that your employer will make up the difference. He may leave you entirely to your own devices in which case you might find it difficult to replace your company pension with a personal pension paid for entirely by your own contributions.

Additional Voluntary Contributions

It may be better if you feel your pension benefits are likely to be lower than you hope for to consider topping up your company pension with Additional Voluntary Contributions (AVCs). You can pay a total of up to 15% of your salary into your pension and the excess over your current contributions can be used to boost your pension by taking out an AVC scheme. AVCs are similar to all other forms of pension contributions in that you get tax relief at your highest rate of income tax and your contributions are invested in tax free funds.

Until 1987 it was not compulsory for an employer to allow you to make AVCs, now he is obliged to. At one time he could also insist that you invest your AVCs in the main pension fund. Now you are able to decide where your AVCs are invested by affecting a Free Standing AVC plan (FSAVC).

Changing jobs

One problem with company pension schemes is what happens when you change jobs. Unless you have less than two years service, you will not get your contributions back, but you will have a choice of what should happen to them. These choices are:

- Leave your contributions invested with your old employer's pension scheme. Your employer is obliged to re-value your pension benefits in line with inflation or by 5% per annum whichever is less.
- Alternatively you may ask for a transfer value which you can invest in your new employer's pension scheme. But the pension benefits you get may be less than those you had before.
- A transfer value could instead be switched into a personal pension policy where the benefits will depend on investment performance but could well be better than you would get from either leaving the money in your old scheme or transferring to your new employer.
- You could use your transfer value to purchase a 'buy-out bond' from an insurance company like a personal pension policy, the final benefits from such a bond will depend on investment performance.

Deciding between these options is not easy and the best thing to do is to get good professional advice.

Summing up

- Remember it is only while you are working that you are able to build up your retirement income. So find out how much pension you can expect from your current pension arrangements.
- If you are self employed you will only get the basic state pension so making your own arrangements is vital. If you already have a Section 226 policy issued prior to 1 July 1988 you can continue to contribute to it, or you can take out a personal pension policy.
- If you are a member of the State Earnings Related Pension Scheme (SERPS) consider opting out if you are young. But remember that it may be a good idea to opt back in at a later date. If not, consider topping up your pension benefits with a Personal Pension Plan if you are not in a company scheme or by Additional Voluntary Contributions ('Free standing' or as part of the employer's scheme) if you are in pensionable employment.
- If you are a member of a company pension scheme, think very carefully before opting out into a personal pension plan. You could lose the security of a pension related to your final salary and you may lose other benefits such as life assurance and widow's benefits. Your employer may not be prepared to contribute to a personal pension plan. If you are a member of a non-contributory pension scheme, it would be particularly unwise. However, if you are young and intend to change your job several times, a personal pension may be a good idea.

8 Saving tax on your income and investments

Though taxes have come down dramatically in recent years, none of us likes paying more tax than we need to. There are various ways in which you can avoid paying too much tax on your income and a number of saving and investment vehicles that are attractive because of their tax treatment.

However, it would be unwise to make a decision about your income or an investment solely for tax reasons without considering other implications. For example, some tax efficient investments such as Personal Equity Plans can be risky and you will need to decide whether you want to take this risk. If an investment goes down in value, the tax concessions are of little use.

When it comes to saving tax on income, the self employed often have the most scope. They can offset a variety of business expenses against income. If you are in this position it usually pays to employ an accountant to make sure you claim all your entitlements. Remember you can also offset your accountant's fees against tax.

But if you are employed a thorough check of your tax position can also reveal ways of saving tax. The first step is to check that you are claiming all the personal reliefs and allowances to which you are entitled.

The main reliefs are:

● Personal allowance

- Married couple's allowance
- Additional personal allowance for children (if you maintain a child but don't qualify for married couple's allowance, eg single parent)
- Blind person's allowance (if either you or your wife is blind)
- Age allowance: 65–74 married/single
  74 or over married/single
- Widow's bereavement allowance (applicable in tax year of spouse's death and following tax year, except on remarriage)

Always inform the tax man immediately of any change in your circumstances. And there is no harm, for example, in reminding him when you or your spouse are about to reach 65 to ensure that you get age allowance promptly in that tax year.

Independent taxation

On 6 April 1990 independent taxation was introduced. Besides giving married women responsibility for completing their own tax returns, independent taxation has provided a number of opportunities for married couples to save tax.

Many of the savings stem from the fact that everybody now receives a personal allowance, with higher allowances for the over 65's, to set off against any income they receive. There is also a married couple's allowance which will normally go to husbands but if a husband is on a low income and the wife is earning more he can pass the allowance to her.

Under the old system a married woman's investment income was taxed as her husband's at his highest rate of income tax. Under the current system, she can offset her personal allowance against her investment income. This means if she is not working or earning enough to absorb her personal

allowance she will be able to receive investment income free
of tax.

If a wife does not currently have enough of her own
investment income to take advantage of this favourable tax
situation, it makes sense for a husband to transfer some of
his taxed investments or jointly held assets into his wife's
name so that she can receive the income free of tax. On
current tax allowances, this could mean a saving of up to
£751 per year for basic rate taxpayers. To achieve these
savings it will, though, be necessary to ensure that the money
is invested either where no tax is deducted from the income,
or where tax can be reclaimed. Life insurance products, such
as investment bonds, are unsuitable as tax is automatically
paid by the insurance company.

Even where a wife is a taxpayer a transfer of investments
could save tax if she pays tax at a lower rate than her husband.
Both husband and wife now receive a basic rate tax allowance
instead of having their income lumped together. Another
good reason for a transfer is if a couple has assets which are
likely to produce capital gains. Under the old system a
married couple only had one annual capital gains tax
exemption between them, now they have one each. So they
can now have gains of up to £10,000 per year tax free.
Naturally, if a wife is the wealthier partner the same
arguments would favour transfers to a husband.

It may not be necessary to transfer an asset completely to the
other partner. Where an asset is held jointly, the taxman
will normally assume that it is owned in equal shares and the
income will be taxed accordingly. But couples can decide to
split the ownership in other proportions, say, 70–30 so that
the wife gets a larger share of the income. You will need to
obtain *Form 17: Declaration of Beneficial Interests* from your
tax office for this purpose. Another area where tax savings
may be possible is on your mortgage. Where there is a joint
mortgage the taxman will normally split the tax relief equally
between you. If one partner is a higher rate taxpayer,
however, you will save more tax if all the relief goes to that

partner. The taxman will allow you to transfer all the relief to one partner, regardless of the fact that it is a joint mortgage, if you complete a *Form 15: Allocation of Interest Election.*

Fringe benefits

If you are employed, there are various ways in which your employer may be able to help you save tax if you can persuade him to give you some of your salary in the form of perks which are not as heavily taxed as ordinary income.

Some perks are completely free of tax, such as:

- work place nurseries
- interest free loans, where the interest would not have exceeded £200
- free or subsidised canteen meals for all employees
- luncheon vouchers up to 15p a day
- working clothing, eg overalls

Other perks, such as private medical insurance and company cars are normally taxable unless you earn less than £8,500 pa, and you are not a company director. But even if you are taxed on them, perks can still be worth having. Their real value often exceeds the tax payments.

Remember if you do have a company car you can keep the tax bill down by clocking up more than 2,500 miles of business mileage in order to avoid the 50% extra tax charge on top of scale rates for 'insubstantial' business use. If you drive 18,000 miles or more on business the scale charge is halved.

Profit related pay

You could suggest that your employer introduces a profit
related pay scheme. Under this scheme, which came into effect
in 1987, half of your profit related pay is totally free of income
tax up to the point where it is 20% of your PAYE pay or
£4,000 a year, if lower. It can either be based on a stated
percentage of the company's profits or be a fixed sum that
varies in proportion with future profits.

Profit related pay can replace a portion of existing salary or
be introduced instead of a pay increase. Tax relief is given
by your employer through the PAYE system. Schemes must
be registered in advance with the Inland Revenue in order
to qualify.

Tax efficient savings and investments

One obvious way to avoid or minimise tax on your savings
and investments is to invest for capital gains and to make
use of your annual capital gains tax allowance. You pay no
tax at all on any gains which fall within the limit. From 1990
married men and women each enjoy a CGT allowance of
£5,000. You can often make sure that you take advantage of
your annual allowance even if you do not intend to sell your
investments by 'bed and breakfasting' your share or unit
trust holdings. This means you sell them one day and buy
them the next.

There are also a number of savings and investment schemes
which enjoy various tax concessions. Those that have already
been covered in detail in previous chapters are summed up
below:

• The most essential of all the tax efficient investments are, of course, pension plans (see Chapter 7). Not only do your pension contributions qualify for tax relief at your highest rate of income tax, but they are invested in tax free funds. At retirement you can take part of your pension as a tax free lump sum.

- TESSAs, to be launched on 1 January 1991, allow deposits in banks and building societies to earn interest tax free over five years (see Chapter 6).
- Personal Equity Plans (PEPs) enable you to invest in shares and enjoy any profits completely free of tax. PEPs are dealt with in more detail later in this chapter.
- National Savings offers Savings Certificates and the Yearly Plan (see Chapter 6) give guaranteed, tax free returns over five years. If you are prepared to gamble you could also consider Premium Bonds, where prizes are tax free, and you are at least guaranteed your stake back.
- Building societies offer SAYE plans (see Chapter 6) which also give guaranteed, tax free returns over five or seven years.
- Low Coupon and Index Linked Gilts (see Chapter 6) are attractive because capital gains are tax free.
- With profits and unit linked endowments (see Chapter 6) are tax efficient savings media for higher rate taxpayers. Investment income within insurance policies is treated as that of the life company and is therefore taxed at the maximum rate of 25% making it more attractive than direct investment in the same assets. Pay-outs are tax free provided they are qualifying policies and policies have been held for at least ten years or three quarters of the term if less.
- Tax exempt friendly society plans (see Chapter 6) are also worth considering.
- Higher rate taxpayers with lump sums to invest could use investment bonds (see Chapter 6). These are attractive if you are likely to be able to defer cashing in the bond until a time when you are paying a lower rate of tax, such as after retirement. As with endowments, tax on investment income within the bond is limited to that incurred by the life office. Another tax advantage is that no capital gains tax is incurred on switches between

investment funds and unit trusts within the bond. A provision for CGT is made in the price of the bond but normally at less than the full rate.

An investment bond also provides a way for higher rate taxpayers to boost their income without paying tax. Annual withdrawals of 5% of the original investment can be made for up to 20 years with no immediate tax liability. If withdrawals are missed, their cumulative total can be taken without tax in further years, eg if no withdrawals are made for five years then 25% could be taken free of tax in one withdrawal.

Other tax efficient saving and investment schemes

Low risk

Save-As-You-Earn Share Option Schemes

The object of these schemes is to help you buy shares in your company. A fixed monthly amount is deducted from your pay for five years and you are then paid a tax free bonus. If you leave your money a further two years you receive another bonus. While you are saving, your money is deposited in either a National Savings, bank or building society account where it earns a fixed rate of interest.

When you join a scheme you are given the option to buy a fixed number of shares in your company with the proceeds of your plan. The great attraction is that the price of the shares is that ruling at the time you start your plan and may even be cheaper. Employers can give a discount of up to 20%. There is no obligation on you to buy the shares and if their price has gone down when your savings plan matures there would be no point in doing so. You can simply take the cash proceeds of the plan. However, if the price of the shares has risen you could buy them and resell them immediately at a profit. No income tax is payable on this gain except with some old schemes. If you decide to hold on to the shares and sell them later a capital gains tax liability may arise. There is little risk in this scheme until you acquire the shares, which may then fluctuate in price.

High risk

Personal Equity Plans

Personal Equity Plans (PEPs) enable you to invest up to £6,000 in shares without incurring any income tax or capital gains tax on your returns. Up to £3,000 of a PEP can be invested in unit trusts or investment trusts which are at least 50% invested in the UK. If this condition is not fulfilled, only £900 can be invested in the fund.

PEPs are offered by a wide variety of financial institutions including banks, building societies, insurance companies, stockbrokers and unit trust groups. You can normally choose between a unit trust or investment trust only PEP or a managed PEP where the managers decide which shares to buy and sell on your behalf. If you choose a managed PEP it is a good idea to look at the manager's track record before making your choice. Normally between three and ten shares are included in a discretionary PEP. Part of your investment may also be put into unit trusts or investment trusts.

Most managed PEPs are invested in the shares of leading Blue Chip companies, but a number of alternative schemes are also available investing, say, in smaller companies, or 'ethical' investments only.

Under some schemes investors can make their own choice of shares, though normally from a pre-selected list.

It is also possible for new issue shares including privatisation issues and issues of shares in building societies converting to plc status to be placed in a PEP. This must be done within 30 days of the share allocation being announced.

For anybody who invests in shares, unit trusts or investment trusts, PEPs are a must. If you don't take up your annual allowance it means you are paying tax unnecessarily.

Offshore funds and UCITS

These are pooled investment funds, operating on the lines of unit trusts or investment trust companies. Originally offshore funds were mainly sold from tax havens such as the Channel Islands, the Isle of Man and Luxembourg. Now any European investment group can offer their funds to UK investors if they are approved as UCITS or directly by the Securities and Investment Board.

Besides investing in shares, these funds offer some investment opportunities not available among onshore funds, such as investment in currencies. They include umbrella funds which allow investors to switch between a range of sub-funds, investing in different currencies or equity markets, while remaining within one fund. These funds can be attractive to both UK and non-resident investors because no tax is deducted from their income at source. UK residents are, however, liable to tax on any income that is paid out and on any gains when switches are made or when the fund is sold.

However, it is very important to note that unless a fund originates from one of the so-called 'Designated Territories', ie the Channel Islands, Isle of Man or Bermuda, investors are not covered by a compensation fund if the investment fund goes bust.

Business Expansion Schemes

In order to encourage investors to take the risk of backing new and growing companies, the Government introduced the Business Expansion Scheme. If you invest in shares in companies through this scheme you get full tax relief on your investment. Thus even if your stake does not appreciate in value, you may still get a good return because of the tax relief. Providing you hold the shares for at least five years, any capital gains that arise when you sell will also be free of capital gains tax. The minimum that can be invested is normally around £1,000 and the maximum is £40,000.

When it was first introduced, investing through the BES was very risky because you were often asked to back new companies with no track record, though you could minimise your risk somewhat by investing in a BES fund which invests in a range of companies. New companies can be very successful but if they go bust you will lose money. And losses on BES cannot be set against other gains unless tax relief is withdrawn.

Since 1988, however, BES schemes have become available that are less risky. They offer shares in businesses which invest in residential property for letting. So even if the company goes bust, the value of the property which it holds should mean that you don't lose all your money. If residential property prices continue to rise as they have done in the past, subject to some short-term hiccups, you could make healthy gains and enjoy an income from this type of scheme. Whichever type of BES you invest in though, your money will effectively be locked away for at least five years. And it is important to find out what provisions the company has made to let you cash in your stake thereafter.

Since no trustees are necessary with these schemes, be sure to stick to those sponsored by reliable financial bodies. They are generally advertised in the press in the Spring and in September to take advantage of tax deadlines. Look out for press comment.

Property Enterprise Zones

There are substantial tax advantages to be gained from investing in commercial properties (ie offices, shops, factories and warehouses) that are situated in Enterprise Zones. A Capital allowance of 100% is given on your investment, excluding land costs, which means you get tax on 90–95% of the money you invest. If you borrow the money to invest you can also get tax relief on the interest set against the rents you recieve from the property. This means that higher rate taxpayers can make this investment at virtually no cost at all. If they borrow the 'after tax relief' cost, the rents should largely cover the interest due on the loan. When you sell your investment, however, it will liable to capital gains tax. Property enterprise trusts have been set up to pool investors' money and acquire portfolios of properties in order to spread the risk. The disadvantage is that such an investment is not easily sold. Investors may be locked in for up to 25 years.

Lloyd's

Becoming a member of Lloyd's, the London insurance market, has been a long-standing means of investment with tax advantages for wealthy individuals, although in recent years a number of scandals has robbed it of some of its kudos. Heavy losses by some syndicates and a reduction in tax concessions have also made it less attractive. However, the basic attraction of being able to get a second return on your investments remains. And most members of Lloyd's who have chosen their syndicates carefully and spread their risks around do very well.

If you want to become a member of Lloyds you have to prove a net worth of at least £250,000, and you will be subjected to a means test to establish the amount of your readily realisable assets, such as shares, property (not your main residence), cash on deposit and surrender values of life policies. Shares in private companies, jewellery and antiques are not included, although in the event of a substantial claim arising against the syndicate or syndicates you join, your whole personal estate will be at risk.

Every member of Lloyd's is required to deposit cash or investments with the Corporation of Lloyd's which it holds as trustee. But any income arising from this money remains that of the members. The deposit will determine the premium limit which can be underwritten by the member in any year. So if you make a profit on your underwriting business you effectively get a double return on your deposit.

An entrance fee and annual contribution to Lloyd's Central Fund are also required.

There are several tax benefits of being a member of Lloyd's. Since it is considered a trade, you can set off any losses you make against other income for that year, and most expenses connected with your membership are also allowed except the entrance fee. Tax relief at your highest rate is given on profits (within certain limits) paid into reserve funds set up to cover you in bad years.

For inheritance tax purposes, as your Lloyds membership is considered a business you will also qualify for 50% business property relief after two years.

Nevertheless, it is important to consider carefully the risk of unlimited liability which comes with being a member of Lloyd's. Getting professional advice before joining is essential.

Summing up

- Make sure you are claiming all the tax allowances to which you are entitled.
- If you have self employed earnings, consider employing an accountant to get you the best tax deal.
- Make sure that you and your spouse are getting the full benefit of independent taxation.
- Take advantage of fringe benefits which are less heavily taxed than additional income.
- Consider investment and savings schemes on their own merits; do not use tax efficiency as your only yardstick.

9 Your children

Having children brings many pleasures and rewards but is also a very expensive business. However, most of us would like to give our children the best start in life that we can afford. Apart from supporting them from day to day, this may involve paying for a private school, maintaining them through higher education, providing them with a nest egg for when they reach adulthood and ensuring they benefit (rather than the taxman) from our money after our death. We may want to do the same for our grandchildren too.

Children's savings and saving for children

An important point to remember when dealing with children's savings is that like adults, children have their own personal tax allowance so providing their income stays below that level they do not have to pay tax.

Until now this meant that building society accounts were not the best place for any money that a child received from friends and relatives or earned from their paper round because tax was deducted at source and could not be reclaimed. The National Savings Investment Account or Capital Bond were better because interest is paid gross. However, from April 1991 it will be possible for non-taxpayers to receive interest from bank and building society accounts free of tax so they will become more attractive homes for children's savings.

However, it is important to note that money given to children by their own parents is taxed differently. Apart from the first £5, any income from this money will still be treated as that of the parents and taxed as such. A way round this is to use tax free investments such as National Savings Certificates or the National Savings Yearly Plan. A TESSA (see Chapter 6) cannot be taken out for a child but savings could be accumulated in one and passed to the child later. Encouraging children to put money aside and save for something they want will teach them a valuable lesson for later life.

Long term saving for children

If you want to build up a nest egg for a child, an investment offering potential capital growth will give the best chance of outpacing inflation over a longer term. A unit linked or with profits endowment, or a tax exempt friendly society plan can be put in trust for when the child reaches, say 18 or 21. But greater flexibility is offered by a unit trust savings plan which can be designated with the child's name. There is no fixed saving period within unit trust savings plans. When a lump sum of £500 to £1000 has been accumulated you can stop saving and leave the money invested. The child can take over the unit holding when he or she reaches 18. Even more tax efficient is for an adult to save money in a Personal Equity Plan on a child's behalf. All the investment income and capital gains within a PEP are tax free.

School fees

Private schooling continues to increase in popularity, but it does not get any cheaper. School fees have been rising steadily over the years at more than the rate of inflation and few parents can afford to pay for them completely out of current income. How much you can do to mitigate the burden will be largely determined by how soon you need the fees and how much you can afford to put aside in advance. But there is little doubt that the earlier you start planning the more affordable it will be. Both regular savings and lump sums can be invested to help fund future fees.

Table 1
How school fees have risen

	% *Average rise in fees*★	RPI
1985	9	5.7
1986	11	3.7
1987	11	3.7
1988	11	6.8
1989	10	7.7

★ Source: Independent Schools Information Service

Regular saving for school fees

If you want to start putting money aside regularly towards the cost of school fees, the time factor will determine the most appropriate schemes to use.

If there are still ten years or more to go until school fees are required then a series of with profits endowments can be used maturing in consecutive years to pay each year's fees as they fall due. Premium payments can be tailored to fit parents' circumstances, for example plans are available where contributions start off low and rise over several years in line with increasing income expectations. The advantage of with profits endowments is that the build up is fairly predictable. Loans can also be taken on the policies if they haven't quite reached maturity.

If there are at least five years to go you could use a new TESSA when they become available in January 1991. This will enable you to accumulate interest in a bank or building society free of tax. But greater gains may be achieved through investing in an income unit trust through a PEP where returns are also tax free. Income can be paid out on a termly basis when the fees become due. But the risks of investing in shares should not be forgotten. PEPs should only form part of your school fees planning.

For shorter periods and to reduce risk National Savings products and building society high interest accounts can be used.

Lump sum investment for school fees

For lump sums there are a variety of investment schemes to consider. At the safest end of the risk spectrum you could use index linked gilts which would guarantee the purchasing power of your capital. Where feasible you could buy a series of these gilts with maturity dates to match the dates when fees will be due. Lump sums of up to £3,000 in year one and £9,000 altogether over a five year period can be invested in a bank or building society TESSA free of tax from January 1991.

Alternatively you could invest in a Personal Equity Plan (PEP). Amounts of up to £6,000 a year can be invested. To keep risks down, choose a plan where the first £3,000 is put into a unit trust or investment trust and the remainder goes into a selection of Blue Chip shares. But bear in mind the risk of stock market fluctuations. Money should be invested in a PEP at least five years before it is needed.

For shorter periods and greater security, you could consider investment in an educational trust if interest rates are high. Here an annuity is purchased which will start making termly payments for school fees at the required date in the future. This method is particularly tax efficient for high rate taxpayers because the charitable status of the trusts enables the trusts to reclaim income tax deducted from the taxable element of the

annuity payments. The school to which the fees must be
paid need not be specified until just before the child is due
to start.

Educational trusts can bring savings even when fees are due
to start immediately, but once again the earlier the investment
can be made the greater the saving. Most annuities are written
on a non-profit basis so the fees provided are fixed at the
time you invest. They can be level or escalate at an agreed
percentage each year, while in payment. This sort of trust
can be good value if annuity rates are high and fees are due
to start fairly soon. However, if there are still three to five
years to go a unit linked or with profits annuity could produce
better returns because payments will reflect investment growth.

Another tax benefit of an educational trust for a parent or
guardian is that the money invested will fall outside his estate
for inheritance tax purposes even if he dies within seven years.
Other adults do not get this advantage, however, unless they
waive their right to cash in their plan.

Another way to use a lump sum is to pay fees in advance to
a school where a composition fee scheme is offered. Here
parents get a discount on fees charged, and the lump sum is
used by the school to purchase an annuity. This type of
scheme has the same tax advantages as the educational trust
schemes, but without the flexibility. It means the parents
are tied to educating their children at a particular school and
problems may arise if for some reason you want to move
them.

Borrowing to finance school fees

Many parents either fail to plan in advance for school fees or
their provision turns out to be inadequate and they may be
forced to borrow money.

The best solution to this problem is usually to take out an
additional mortgage on the family home. Various schemes are

available which normally allow parents to borrow between 75% and 85% of their property value less any outstanding mortgage. Once the facility is arranged the loan can usually be drawn down as it is needed to pay fees and interest is only charged on the money that has actually been borrowed. However, the interest rate may be slightly higher than for a standard mortgage scheme. The capital will be repayable at the end of a set period of 10 to 25 years normally from the proceeds of an endowment or pension plan policy.

The advantage of these loan schemes is their flexibility. You are not tied to using the money for school fees provision. It can also be used to support children in higher education, or for other purposes.

However, there is no doubt that funding school fees through loans is a much more expensive alternative than saving in advance.

Inheritance tax

Few of us would like the idea of the taxman getting any of our money when we die, but many people still fail to make any provision for inheritance tax (IHT) because they do not feel they are wealthy enough to be affected by it. Their children often have to pay the price for this neglect. Despite regular annual increases in the starting level of the tax, rising house prices alone can push people's estates over the limit. IHT currently applies to estates worth over £128,000 and the rate is 40p in the pound.

If your children are landed with an inheritance tax bill after you die this can cause considerable problems. They may, for example, be forced to sell the family home or other possessions, which they would have liked to keep, in order to raise the money for the taxman.

So it is well worth looking at ways in which you may be able to avoid or reduce a potential IHT bill or, failing that, make some provision for its payment.

Part of your estate will, of course, fall below the level at which tax starts. This is known as the 'nil rate' band, and there are ways in which it can be used several times over. There are also concessions which allow some gifts to be made completely free of IHT.

Transfers between husband and wife, whether during their lifetime or when one dies, are free of tax, and so is normal expenditure from income. There is an annual exemption of £3,000, which can be given away each year, and a small gifts exemption of £250. Gifts on the marriage of children or grandchildren are also exempt within given limits.

The question of passing on a business will be dealt with in the next chapter.

Other outright gifts during your lifetime can be made free of tax (with some exceptions) but if you die within seven years of making them a liability may then arise. For this reason, they are known as Potentially Exempt Transfers (PETS). A gift made within three years of your death will be subject to the full rate of tax, but after that the tax tapers off. You could make provision against a possible tax bill arising on such transfers by taking out decreasing term assurance but this is really only of value if you are making very substantial gifts. Gifts made more than seven years before death are ignored for IHT purposes.

An obvious way to avoid IHT is, therefore, to give away as much of your money as you can at least seven years before death. But this may not always be practicable.

Minimising inheritance tax

Married couples may be able to minimise IHT on their deaths by 'estate equalisation'. This enables the 'nil rate' band, ie the amount below the £128,000 to be used twice over. Thus, instead of one partner leaving all of his or her assets tax free to the other on death and then the whole lot passing to the children on the second death with a large tax bill to pay, the assets are passed on in easy stages. Firstly, husband and wife should transfer assets to each other during their lifetime free of tax and then arrange that as each of them dies part of each of their estates is passed on to the children within the 'nil rate' band.

If a husband or wife has died within the last two years without leaving assets to adult children, or has left assets which exceeded the 'nil rate band', the surviving family could consider varying the interests under the will by a 'deed of family arrangement' so that some assets are passed on but not more than the 'nil rate band'.

One problem, though, is that much of many people's wealth is tied up in their home. Under present IHT rules, it is not possible to reduce your estate by making a lifetime gift of your home to your children if one or both of you continue to live there. Unless you pay a full market rent for the use of the property it will still be treated as part of your estate on death.

Passing on your home before death is therefore often not practical. But it is worth noting that in order to ease the tax burden, IHT payable in respect of a gift of property, either during lifetime or on death, can be paid by ten annual instalments.

For the over 65s who continue to need income from their capital, an effective and immediate method of saving IHT is what is known as a 'back-to-back' plan. This involves purchasing an annuity that provides regular payments, part of which is used to provide the investor with some income and the remainder to pay the premiums on a minimum cost whole life policy to provide a lump sum on your death. By purchasing the annuity your estate is automatically reduced in value, which means a lower tax bill. This reduction in tax liability plus the payout on the life policy should more than recompense your heirs for the money that you have invested in the annuity. If the life policy is put in trust for your heirs no tax will be payable on the proceeds.

Making provision for the IHT bill

If you either cannot afford to or find it impractical to give away your money before you die, you may instead want to help your heirs by providing them with some assistance in meeting the eventual IHT bill so they are not forced to sell off your possessions. This can be done through a life assurance policy and providing it has been put in trust its value will not actually be included in your estate when IHT is calculated.

Since there is no way of knowing when death will occur a whole life insurance policy is preferable, normally paying out on the second death in the case of married couples. The earlier you can take out the policy the better value you will get since otherwise advancing age and poor health will automatically push up your premiums. A unit linked or with profits whole life policy may be used.

Trusts

When you are making financial plans for your family, trusts can be a very useful tool.

It usually makes sense for insurance policies taken out for protection purposes to be covered by some form of appropriate trust so that your family can receive the proceeds straightaway without having to wait for probate.

The proceeds of such policies will not form part of your estate either if your trust is worded correctly so they are also useful in inheritance tax planning.

One sort of trust is that written under the provisions of the Married Women's Property Act 1882. These are simple trusts for the benefit of your husband or wife and/or children, and they have certain advantages in the event of a bankruptcy. However, many insurance companies now make available more flexible trusts which allow you to include a wider class of beneficiaries.

It also makes sense for most pension policies to be written in trust in case of death before retirement in order to ensure the benefit is not subject to IHT.

If you are a high rate taxpayer and you want to put money aside for when your children have grown up it is worth considering setting up an accumulation and maintenance trust. By doing so, besides avoiding IHT (providing you survive seven years) you can also avoid having to pay higher rate tax yourself on any income arising from your gift which would otherwise be the case. However, for this formula to work the income must be accumulated for each child until at least the age of 18 and no payments should be made for their benefit until they reach that age.

Income within the trust will be subject to basic rate tax and an additional rate of tax making a total rate of 35% at present. For this reason it is often a good idea to invest the money in an endowment or investment bond where any income will be taxed at more favourable rates within the insurance policy itself.

Normally such trusts come to an end when your children are between the ages of 18 and 25 and the accumulated value is shared out between them. This money will be treated as capital in the hands of the child and no higher rate tax will be payable on the accumulated income. However, if you do not want your children to have the capital then you can give them a right to the income instead. The capital can be distributed later on.

Normally an accumulation and maintenance trust must end within 25 years, unless all the beneficiaries have a common grandparent. There is no distinction made between legitimate, illegitimate and adopted children.

Summing up

- Remember that children are normally non-taxpayers, providing their income remains within their personal tax allowance, so their savings are often best invested where no tax is deducted or where it can be reclaimed.
- Consider tax free or non-income producing investments for any money you give your own children, otherwise you could be liable for tax on the interest.
- Start planning for school fees as early as possible. Use your home to raise money for school fees or to support children through higher education if you need to borrow.
- Check your inheritance tax position and take steps to minimise your liability, or to provide your heirs with funds to meet the bill. Put money in trust where appropriate

10 Your business

The number of people moving into self employment and setting up their own businesses has mushroomed in recent years. While it is recognised that planning is necessary to get a business off the ground in the first place, businessmen often become so busy with the day-to-day running of their business that they fail to give further thought to the future.

Failure to plan can, however, cause just as many problems for a business as it can in your personal life. For example, it could mean that your business pays more tax than it needs to. The possible death of a partner or another key person within the organisation can have a crippling effect unless provision is made in advance.

You must also think forward to the time when you will want to retire. Many small businessmen believe they will continue working indefinitely, but find when they get older that they would like to work less but cannot afford to. They assume they will be able to sell their business and provide for their retirement from the proceeds. When they reach retirement, however, they find that their business does not fetch as much as they had expected.

Setting up in business

One of the first decisions you will have to make when you are setting up in business is whether you intend to operate as a sole trader, partnership or as a limited company. This will affect your tax position.

As a sole trader you are treated as self employed. This can have various tax advantages. Any initial losses can be offset against your previous years' earnings as an employee, and the first two or three years' tax assessments can be based on your opening year's profits. A disadvantage, however, is that you are fully liable for all your debts and your personal assets may also have to be used to satisfy business debts.

A partnership consists of a group of self employed people. It can have various advantages such as enabling the pooling of resources and ideas. Distribution of profits within the partnership can be made with tax planning in mind. However, you will still have unlimited liability at a personal level and each partner will be responsible for the full debts of the partnership.

By setting up a company, which can be bought off the shelf for around £150 or so, you have the advantage that your liability is limited only to the capital you have put into the company, unless you have provided personal guarantees as well. On the other hand, you will have to fulfil various official requirements, such as filing audited accounts at Companies House each year.

It would be well worth your while discussing the pros and cons of each of these forms of business with an accountant and solicitor before you make your final decision.

Whichever way you decide to trade, if you are married involving your spouse in your business can be a good way of saving tax if he or she is a non-taxpayer or pays tax at a lower rate than you. Even if your spouse is not able to work in the business, you could make him or her a sleeping partner or shareholder and divide the profits or dividends accordingly.

Assuring the future of your business

The future of any business often rests just as heavily on the health of its managers and key workers as it does on external factors.

In a partnership, the death of a partner can have serious implications not just because he or she will no longer be making an input into the business but because his or her dependants are very likely to need to withdraw that partner's capital and assets from the business to provide for their future. This could mean that the remaining partners are forced to sell assets or borrow money in order to buy out their deceased partner's share causing considerable problems to all concerned or even mean that the business has to be wound up.

Such problems can be avoided if each member of a partnership is insured for an appropriate sum so that if one dies the business has enough to pay off the widow and dependants. However, careful thought should be given to how the policy is written in order to avoid a tax charge when the proceeds are paid.

Various types of insurance policy can be used for this purpose. A term assurance policy could be used to provide cover cheaply for a specific period, or alternatively a unit linked whole life policy. The latter has the advantage of providing flexibility. Sums assured can be altered if necessary and the policy will normally acquire a surrender value according to the growth of the fund in which the premiums are invested. So if a partner survives until retirement, the policy can be cashed in and the proceeds used to help buy out his share of the business at retirement.

Insuring the life of a key employee can be equally important. For example, if somebody such as a sales manager, dies in the middle of some important negotiations, it could mean the loss of a valuable contract and a loss of profits as well. The proceeds of a life policy could help to compensate for this loss.

Providing sick pay can be burdensome for a small business, though sometimes morally difficult to refuse, so it is also a good idea to set up a group Permanent Health Insurance scheme, or encourage individuals to take out their own policies.

Retiring from your business

If you are relying on money from the sale of your business or being bought out by your partners in order to provide for your retirement, think again, you could be in for a disappointment. Your own retirement could in itself reduce the value of your business significantly and there may be other factors beyond your control which reduce the price you get.

It is more certain and tax efficient to make proper pension provision in advance.

Pension contributions attract tax relief at your highest rate of tax. And if your company makes contributions, these can reduce its profits and hence the amount of corporation tax payable. Pension funds are free of UK income tax and capital gains tax, and can therefore grow faster than other taxed forms of saving. At retirement, you can take part of your pension as a lump sum and the rest will be taxed as earned income.

More details about personal pension plans can be found in Chapter 7.

Some self employed people may resist committing themselves to a pensions contract in case their income fluctuates and they cannot keep up their contributions. But this need not be a worry because contributions can take the form of single premiums which can vary from year to year. What's more, regular premium contracts nowadays tend to be highly flexible too.

In a partnership, each partner can take out his or her own personal pension plan. If a wife is working in her husband's business, it also makes sense for her to take out her own personal pension plan scheme.

If you are able to take out a personal pension you can also take out inexpensive life assurance where tax relief can be claimed on the premiums. This can be useful in partnership planning.

If you have a company you can, as an alternative to a personal pension plan, take out an executive pension scheme for yourself and other directors and key employees. Company contributions to an executive scheme rank as a business expense for tax purposes within certain limits and can be offset against taxable profits, thereby enabling the company tax bill to be reduced and the money to be channelled into your pension scheme instead. Employees can contribute up to 15 per cent of their earnings and receive income tax relief at their highest rate.

With an executive pension scheme there are limits on the pension benefits. After a minimum of 20 years service with the company, a maximum pension of two-thirds final salary can be taken. Final salary for this purpose, though, is subject to an overall ceiling, currently of £64,800, which will be revised each year in line with the RPI. A tax-free lump sum of up to 2.25 times salary can be taken.

Loan facilities

Several years ago many small businessmen were reluctant to put money into pension schemes and lock it away until retirement in case they developed cash flow problems. Nowadays, however, most pension schemes offer loan facilities.

Personal loans

A personal loan to a policyholder under a personal or executive pension scheme is normally provided by a third party such as a bank or building society on an interest only basis. Security is usually required in the form of residential property, commercial property, stocks and shares or life insurance policies. The policyholder pays interest to the lender and the capital is repaid at retirement from the tax free cash sum. As well as being useful for house purchase, such loans can also be valuable for other purposes such as school fees.

Company loans

Loanbacks from an executive pension plan to a company are governed by a number of rules. The loan must not exceed 50% of the current value of the plan. It must be for a genuine commercial reason and it must be made on commercial terms at a market rate of interest. The loan must be repaid by the company before the director retires.

The mechanics of the loan differ between insurance companies. Some will transfer the required amount from the pension fund into a special interest bearing account and then lend the company the money at a higher rate of interest, while others simply lend money from the pension fund direct and the interest is credited back to the pension plan.

The combination of the executive pension plan and the loanback can be very tax efficient for a small business as the following example shows:

Example *Company Loans*	*Without executive plan*	*With executive plan*
Company pre-tax profits	£140,000	£140,000
Minus contribution to pension	–	£40,000
Corporation tax due	£35,000	£25,000
Retained profit	£105,000	£75,000
Loanback from executive plan to company	–	£20,000
	£105,000	£95,000

Through the use of the executive plan with the loanback, the amount retained by the company has been reduced by £10,000 but in its place £40,000 has been invested in a tax free executive pension plan.

Small self-administered pension schemes

Another alternative is for a company to set up its own self-administered pension scheme. The attraction of this type of scheme is that it enables the directors to decide investment policy themselves. This can include investing up to 50% of the scheme in your own company but this is only allowed where each member of the scheme is a 20% director and a trustee. Otherwise self investment is limited to 5% of the pension fund. A number of insurance companies offer hybrid self-administered schemes where they undertake the administration and manage part of the pension fund giving the directors control of the remainder.

Even so, self-administered schemes do give directors extra responsibilities and involvement which they may not always want, and often the availability of a loan facility under an executive pension scheme is enough to satisfy most directors' requirements.

Passing on your business

Just as with your personal assets, inheritance tax will also raise its head if you die within seven years of passing on your business. A large inheritance tax bill could prove crippling to a business but fortunately some relief is available to reduce the value of the capital transfer providing you owned the business property for at least two years prior to passing it on.

Business property relief of 50% is given on the transfer of a sole trader's business assets, for a partner's interest in a firm's business, or for a controlling shareholding in a trading company. Property, such as land and buildings, owned by you and used by the partnership or company, attracts relief at 30%. Minority shareholdings only attract relief if the company is unquoted, relief is 50% for shareholdings between 25% and 50%, but is only 30% for smaller shareholdings.

Relief is lost or reduced, however, if the business property or part of it is sold by the recipient before the donor's death, unless it is replaced by other business assets within a year.

Summing up

- When you are setting up your own business, consider carefully the form it should take first with the help of professional advisers.
- Consider insuring the lives of partners or key employees to avoid possible financial problems on their death.
- Don't rely on the sale of your business to provide your retirement income, take out a pension scheme.

11 Planning once you reach retirement

Once you reach retirement your financial priorities change. Instead of building up capital out of income, you will normally be looking for the best ways of investing your capital to provide extra income to supplement your pension.

The mistake that many retired people still make, however, is to think too short term. They tend to aim for the highest income they can get immediately without giving enough thought to the future. It has been pointed out in this book before, but it cannot be stressed enough that even at retirement long term planning is still necessary. It should always be borne in mind that the average life expectancy of a man of 60 is 18.6 years, while a woman of 60 could live until well past 80. Over this length of time, inflation will take its toll on your capital unless you invest it where it has a chance to keep pace. If you don't, the purchasing power of your capital will decline and so too will the value of the income that it provides.

However, this does not mean taking undue risks. Although during your working life you may be able to afford to lose money on a speculative investment because you can, if the worst comes to the worst, build up your capital again out of income, you won't have this second chance at retirement. More than ever at retirement, you should bear in mind that protection of your capital should be your first priority.

It is important therefore to give careful thought to exactly how much income you really need at retirement. The more modest you can be in your requirements initially, the more opportunities you will have to invest your capital in ways which will provide you with a growing income in the future. If you find you have more than enough income, this is a sure sign that your capital could be invested more productively in another form.

You should also remember the need to review your investments during retirement. Once again, too many retired people take the view that after they have invested their money when they first retire, that is where it should stay. But this is not the case. First, because the investment scene is constantly changing so that what may have been a competitive product when you first choose it could be overtaken by better ones. And secondly, because some investments, such as annuities, which are not suitable during early retirement may be worth considering when you are older.

Tax

Unfortunately tax cannot be forgotten when you get to retirement. It is often thought that pensions are tax free, but they are not, even the state pension is taxable. And tax can also play an important part in your choice of investments.

However, thanks to independent taxation which came into effect in April 1990, many retired couples will pay less tax than they did in the past. A married woman now has a personal allowance which can be set off against her pension (even if it is one based on her husband's contributions) and her investment income.

Both husband and wife also receive an extra tax allowance from 65 onwards known as age allowance. A further increase is given at age 75. The married couple's allowance also increases with age. Under independent taxation both husband and wife will receive a capital gains tax allowance of £5,000 each.

In order to get the full benefit of independent taxation, married couples should ensure that the ownership of their investments is divided so that each has a sufficient income to utilise their allowances to the greatest extent possible which means they can receive the maximum amount free of tax. It will also allow them to take advantage of the double CGT allowance. Those with higher incomes will need to arrange that one partner's income remains below the age allowance income limit (currently £12,300) to ensure that the full married age allowance is retained. Single pensioners need to be equally aware of falling into this so-called age allowance trap which works as follows.

If you receive more than the income limit your age allowance is reduced by £1 for every £2 by which your income exceeds the limit until you are left with nothing more than the ordinary tax allowance. The effect is that you end up paying a very high rate of tax on this extra income If you find you are falling into this trap, you will need to consider investments which will help you to avoid it.

How the age allowance trap works

Your income	–	£12,500	
Income limit for Age Allowance (1990/91)	–	£12,300	
Income in Trap		£200	
Reduction in Age Allowance	–	£200 × 1/2	= £100
Extra Tax to Pay			
On Excess Income	–	25% × £200	= £ 50
Due to Loss of Age Allowance	–	25% × £100	= £ 25
Total Extra Tax Paid			= £ 75
Effective tax rate (£75 as a % of £200)			= 37.5%

Your pension at retirement

One of your first decisions at retirement if you are a member of a company pension scheme or have a personal pension plan will be whether you want to take part of your pension as a tax free lump sum. The maximum lump sum you can take varies according to the type of pension scheme to which you belong. There will be several factors which may influence your decision. If you are married you may want to take a lump sum in order to provide your spouse with enough income to utilise his or her personal tax allowance. This may not be necessary but you may have another specific use for the money, such as a special holiday or the purchase of a country cottage. And naturally, if you have a pension related mortgage or another loan outstanding against your pension you will have to take enough cash, within the permitted limits, to repay it. But even if you don't actually need a lump sum, there may still be good reasons for taking one.

However, if you are a member of a company pension scheme there is another factor to take into account. You may be granted a lump sum automatically, but otherwise you should consider how generous your employer has been in increasing the pensions of retired employees before deciding whether to take a lump sum or not. If he has a good record of giving regular increases which have kept pensions in line with or rising faster than inflation, you may be better off not taking a lump sum because there is no guarantee that if you invest the money elsewhere you will get a similarly increasing income. However, if he has not been so generous, taking a lump sum could enable you to invest it more advantageously.

Personal pension policy holders are normally best advised to take a lump sum for tax reasons. This is because while a pension is taxable, the lump sum is tax free and can be invested in a more tax efficient environment. A higher income can normally be achieved by investing the lump sum in an ordinary annuity, for example, because part of the annuity payment is treated as a capital payment and is not taxable.

If you have a personal pension policy, besides deciding on a lump sum you will also need to shop around to find the company with the best annuity rates when you retire so you get the best pension available. You are not restricted to taking a pension from the company you invested with though if you have a pension contract taken out before 1 July 1988 you may end up with a smaller tax free lump sum if you move to a company with which you have no existing contract.

You will also have to weigh up whether you want a pension that is fixed, that escalates at a certain percentage each year, or a pension that is unit linked or with profits. One of the drawbacks of escalating, unit linked or with profit pensions is that they normally start at a lower level than a fixed pension, although in time they should overtake it. Choosing the right type of pension is not easy and will depend partly on how much income you need immediately, and also on your state of health. If you are in poor health a fixed pension will probably give you the best deal as you may not live to enjoy a higher income from the other types.

Investing for income

Even though your choice of investment products will change when you get to retirement, it is still important to aim for a balance in order to protect your capital as discussed in Chapter 6. It is nevertheless likely that your preferred balance will swing more towards fixed interest type investment.

Table 1

Investing for income – Your main choices

Investment	Income	Value of Capital
Annuities	Can be fixed or variable	Normally no return of capital
Building societies/ Banks/TESSAs	Normally variable	Fixed
Gilts	Fixed*	Fixed if held to maturity*
Guaranteed Income Bonds	Fixed	Fixed
Investment Bonds	Fixed**	Variable
National Savings Income Bond	Variable	Fixed
Unit trusts	Variable	Variable
Personal Equity Plans	Variable	Variable

*Can be index linked
**Not strictly income but withdrawals of capital (see text)

Building societies

Building societies will certainly play an important part in your retirement investment strategy. You will need to maintain an emergency fund to meet rainy day requirements, and building societies also offer a range of accounts designed to meet older people's needs for monthly income payments. From April 1991 it will also be possible for non-taxpayers to receive interest paid without tax deducted.

If you are investing for income, instant access to your capital is normally a second priority so it is better to accept a longer notice period of withdrawals in order to qualify for higher interest rates.

Remember to keep a regular check on new accounts and interest rate changes to make sure you are getting the best deal. When your society improves its terms, find out if this applies to existing accounts. This does not always take place automatically.

TESSAs

From 1 January 1991, you will also be able to take advantage of the new Tax Exempt Special Savings Account (TESSA) announced in the 1990 Budget. Through a TESSA you will be able to invest in bank and building societies and all the interest you receive will be completely free of tax providing you leave your capital untouched for five years.

Although early withdrawals of capital will lead to a loss of tax advantages, you will be able to receive the full amount of interest credited to the account less basic rate tax. The balance of the interest will have to be left in the account until the end of the five-year period.

The maximum lump sum deposits into a TESSA will be £3,000 in year one, and up to £1,800 in the following years subject to a total of £9,000 altogether. Husbands and wives can have one each.

After five years the account will cease to be tax exempt but a new account can then be opened and £3,000 transferred across.

Details of how TESSAs will work, such as the rate of interest payable, whether it will be fixed or variable and whether there will be penalties on early withdrawal, are being left to the financial institutions so it will be necessary to shop around for the best deal.

However, unless you only have a small amount of capital keeping too much in a building society is unwise. The two major disadvantages of using building societies to provide income is uncertainty about future interest rates and lack of protection against inflation. Because building society interest rates fluctuate in line with general rates, you have no way of knowing whether your income is likely to go up or down in the future. One point which is certain, though, is that because of inflation the purchasing power of your capital is likely to be gradually eroded.

National Savings

National Savings products can also be attractive sources of income particularly for non-taxpayers until April 1991 when building societies can start paying interest gross, and for those caught in the age allowance trap.

The National Savings Monthly Income Bond is popular with retired people and is especially useful to non-taxpayers because interest is paid without any deduction of income tax. Taxpayers will be liable to tax on the income, however, and should therefore always compare the after-tax return with that being paid by the building societies.

It is also important to bear in mind that withdrawals from an Income Bond can only be made at three months notice, and if a withdrawal is made before the first anniversary of purchase, the rate of interest will be half the published rate. Withdrawals without notice are only allowed on the death of an investor.

As with building society accounts, the income you will get
from an Income Bond will fluctuate in line with general
interest rates.

Another way of obtaining an income from National Savings
that is recommended for higher rate taxpayers or those in
the age allowance trap is to use National Savings Certificates
on which returns are tax free. Since they do not actually pay
out an income, you will need to cash in some of your
certificates each year to supplement your income. However,
it is possible to do this and still end up with an amount
equivalent to your original capital after five years.

Index Linked National Savings Certificates do not provide an
income but are worth including in your portfolio,
particularly in times of high inflation, so that you can be sure
to maintain the purchasing power of at least some of your
capital, without any risk. They pay a guaranteed bonus which
increases over a five-year period on top of index linking.

Gilts

Gilts have already been mentioned earlier in the book as a
source of capital growth. But they are also attractive to
investors who want to be sure of a fixed income for a known
period. They remove the uncertainty which building society
investors face. When interest rates and inflation are rising,
ordinary gilts are not such a good idea, but if your income
requirement is not too high it may be worth considering index
linked gilts, on which the income increases with inflation.
The capital value is also index linked though you can only be
sure of getting the full benefit of this if you hold the stock
until maturity.

If you are buying gilts for income it is important to be aware
of the difference between the quoted interest rate of the

stock, the 'coupon', and the actual yield you get which is determined by the price you pay.

Although gilts are issued in £100 lots, which is their nominal or par value and is the amount the holder receives on redemption, the price you pay for a gilt is rarely the same as the par value. It may be above or below par value, mainly according to the relation of the coupon to current interest rates. If the coupon is higher, then the price is likely to be above par, and vice versa. Buying a gilt that is over par is not recommended because you will suffer a reduction in your capital at redemption.

How to work out the yield on a gilt

To find the flat or running yield you must divide the coupon by the price of the stock and then multiply by 100 to get the percentage figure: eg say that 10.25% Exchequer 1995 is currently priced at £94 then the calculation is:

$$10.25 \div 94 \times 100 = 10.90\%$$

To find out the redemption yield, which takes into account the capital gain or loss of the stock at maturity, you subtract the price from the nominal value and divide the answer by the years to redemption. You then add this figure to, or subtract it from the running yield to produce the redemption yield: eg assume the above stock is purchased in 1990 so there are five years to redemption then the calculation is:

$$6 \div 5 = 1.2$$
$$1.2 + 10.9 = 12.1\%$$

Income on gilts is normally paid twice yearly. If you would like income more frequently you can spread your money around between different gilts with different payment dates. For example, three gilts could provide you with payments every other month, while six would enable you to get a monthly payment.

Buying several gilts is also a good idea because you can stagger

Table 2

Where to buy gilts, the pros and cons

Where to go	Cost	Advantages	Disadvantages
National Savings Stock Register at Post Offices	£1 up to £250- plus 50p for every £125 or part thereafter	Cheap and convenient	No advice, price cannot be specified
Stockbrokers	Usual commission	Advice given on appropriate stock	Expensive if investing small amount
Bank	Stockbrokers' commission plus possible extra admin charge	Advice given on appropriate stock, convenient if you have no stockbroker	Expensive if investing small amount

repayment dates. Otherwise if you have just one gilt paying a high income which matures when interest rates are low your income will fall dramatically. Having, say, three stocks which mature at five year intervals means that when one matures only a third of your income will be affected; it gives you time to make up some ground before the next stock matures. It is not recommended that you buy gilts with more than 15 years to redemption.

Income on gilts is taxable. But if you buy through the National Savings Stock Register at the Post office the interest is paid gross without tax deducted, which is particularly useful for non-taxpayers. Stock bought through other routes will normally have basic rate tax deducted at source before interest is paid, though you can request that it is transferred to the NSSR in order to receive gross payments.

Gilt unit trusts are also available, but since direct investment is straightforward and relatively cheap, there is no particular need to use a unit trust. Moreover, a unit trust cannot pass on to you the favourable tax treatment of gilts.

Guaranteed income bonds

Another source of fixed income are guaranteed income bonds which are issued by insurance companies normally for terms of between one and ten years. At the end of the period, your capital is returned intact. The insurers obtain the income by investing in gilts and other fixed interest securities with maturity dates to match the terms of the bonds. Because the insurance companies can offset their expenses against taxable income, they are often able to offer very competitive interest rates on these bonds.

Income is normally paid once a year, although some companies offer the option of half yearly or monthly payments instead.

Most bonds are now based on single premium whole life or endowment policies with guaranteed bonuses which are cashed in each year to provide the income. This type of bond is particularly tax efficient for older people who are in danger of falling into the age allowance trap because most of the income is not taxable. Only that part of the return which exceeds 5% will be treated as taxable income for age allowance income limit purposes, unlike other investments where the whole of the grossed up equivalent of the net income is taken into account (ie the interest you receive with basic rate tax added back on).

However, a snag can arise on encashment of the bond because all the gain (including the earlier 5% withdrawals) is regarded as part of the income in that tax year. No 'top slicing' is allowed for age allowance purposes. But these disadvantages will normally be more than offset by the tax savings on the income that have been achieved during the period of the bond.

Some guaranteed income bonds are based on a combination of a deferred and immediate temporary annuity. The immediate annuity provides the income, and the deferred annuity provides for the return of the original investment at the end of the period. These can provide good returns for basic rate taxpayers, but for higher rate taxpayers or those faced with the age allowance trap the endowment based bonds are better.

Personal Equity Plans and income unit trusts

Although building society accounts give a high immediate income and gilts and guaranteed income bonds offer the certainty of fixed payments, what most people really need is a growing income. This is not just because living costs are continually being driven up by inflation, but also because as we get older we often need to buy more services, such as help with cleaning and decorating which previously we would have managed ourselves.

The best way of ensuring a rising income is by investing in shares. But unless you have a large capital sum and can achieve a varied portfolio, investing in high yielding shares direct is likely to be too risky and too expensive. One answer is to use income unit trusts which pool investors' money and invest in a large number of high yielding shares thus providing a spread of risk.

You can avoid paying any tax on the income you receive from unit trusts (or other UK shares purchased direct or through investment trusts) if you invest through a Personal Equity Plan (PEP). Any capital gains will also be tax free. Lump sums of up to £3,000 per year can be invested in unit trusts or investment trusts within a PEP. This limit applies to individual investors so a married couple can put in double this amount. A further £3,000 can go direct into shares but because of the limited number involved the risks increase substantially.

If you invest in unit trusts outside a PEP, the income is paid net of basic rate tax, but this can be reclaimed by non-taxpayers. Higher rate taxpayers will have a further tax liability. Capital gains on unit trusts are liable to tax but if they fall within your annual exemption limit you will have no tax to pay.

There are four different basic types of income unit trusts; UK equity income, UK mixed income, gilt and fixed interest, and international income. UK equity income funds invest purely in high yielding ordinary shares. UK mixed income hold a mixture of ordinary shares and fixed interest stock. The gilt and fixed interest funds invest in government securities and company fixed interest and convertible shares. And international income funds invest in overseas shares and fixed interest stock.

The best prospect of a rising income and capital growth are provided by an equity income fund. High yielding shares are usually those of companies which are temporarily out-of-favour. Providing the companies are otherwise sound, their share prices normally recover when they come back into fashion and their yields will fall back. This provides capital growth and means the fund manager will be continually taking profits and seeking out fresh buying opportunities.

Naturally any investment in shares involves risk and there may be times when the capital value of your investment dips. However, since income is your main priority you do not really have to worry. Although share prices fluctuate, dividends tend to show much steadier growth. (These trends are illustrated earlier in the book by the table on page 71.)

The problem with investing in an equity income unit trust is that it means accepting a lower income than you would get, say, from a building society to begin with. But there is a good prospect that within a few years not only will your income overtake and exceed that from a building society, but also that your capital will have appreciated in value. The table on page 151 illustrates this point. Thus, by putting part of your money in an income unit trust, it will help to give you some protection against inflation.

Most unit trusts pay out income twice a year, or sometimes quarterly, but a number of unit trust groups now offer monthly income packages which include four or six trusts so that the investor gets a payment every month. Such a package can include different types of income funds, not just UK trusts but international as well, and fixed interest funds may also be included to boost the overall yield. However, your income will not be level each month as each of the funds will have a different yield.

Although these packages are convenient, to spread your risk it would be a better idea to split your investment across two or three companies' income funds.

Assuming your unit trusts are growing in value, a way of supplementing the income from your unit trusts is to cream off some of the capital gains to top up your income to the required level. An advantage of turning your capital gains into income is that they are tax free, providing you remain within your annual exemption limit. But such a course must be pursued with caution because there is a danger that you could encash your units at a faster rate than they are growing so the value of your investment will fall.

Before you buy any unit trusts always be sure to study a group's past performance record. Don't be too impressed by one or two year figures, look for long term consistency.

Investment trusts

Investment trusts also offer managed portfolios of income shares but the choice of income trusts is more limited than with unit trusts. International and UK income trusts are available. It is also possible to invest up to £3,000 in investment trusts through a PEP.

An advantage of income investment trusts is that many trade at a discount to their true value so you are buying a stream of income more cheaply than investing in the same shares direct or through a unit trust. For example, you may only need to pay £85 to get an income on £100 of shares.

Another option is to invest in the income shares of split capital investment trusts, but these often trade at a premium, so to avoid capital loss you may want to buy the capital shares as well. A stockbroker will be able to advise.

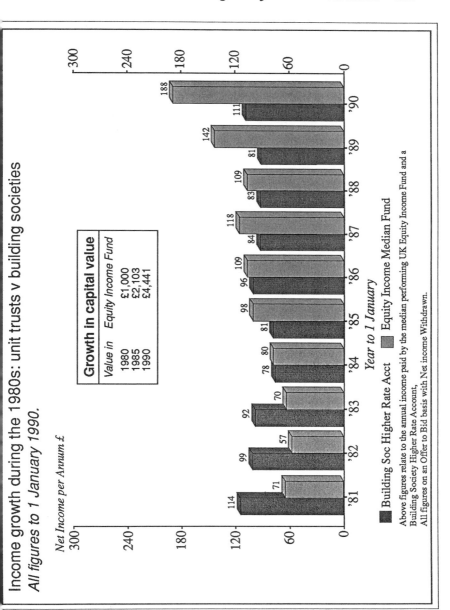

Income growth during the 1980s: unit trusts v building societies
All figures to 1 January 1990.

Net Income per Annum £

Growth in capital value

Value in	Equity Income Fund
1980	£1,000
1985	£2,103
1990	£4,441

Year to 1 January

■ Building Soc Higher Rate Acct   ■ Equity Income Median Fund

Above figures relate to the annual income paid by the median performing UK Equity Income Fund and a Building Society Higher Rate Account,
All figures on an Offer to Bid basis with Net income Withdrawn.

Investment bonds

Investment bonds (also discussed in Chapter 6) can provide
a useful source of income when an investor is a higher rate
taxpayer or falls within the age allowance trap. The advantage
of bonds is that you are allowed to withdraw 5% of your
original investment each year from a single premium bond
and it is not counted as part of your taxable income until
you cash in your bond. So you can boost your income without
boosting your tax bill, or affecting your age allowance. These
withdrawals can be made for up to 20 years, and if any
withdrawals are missed they can be taken in future years,
eg 10% withdrawals every other year. If the withdrawals are
over 5% pa, any excess will be included in your taxable
income and may be subject to higher rate tax.

On encashment the gain from a bond, including previous
withdrawals, will be paid net of basic rate tax but may be
subject to higher rate tax. In order to work out whether
further tax is payable, the gain is 'top-sliced' It is divided
by the number of years the bond has been held. This slice is
then added to the bondholder's income in the year of
encashment. If this puts the investor into a higher rate tax
bracket, then the average rate of tax on the slice is applied
to the whole gain. But if not, the whole gain is free of higher
rate tax.

Annuities

In return for a lump sum investment in an annuity, insurance
companies will provide a guaranteed income for life. The rates
payable on ordinary annuities, which are invested in gilts,
local authority loans and other fixed interest securities, vary
frequently according to current interest rates. A good time to
buy annuities is when interest rates are about to start going

down so you can lock into higher rates. If they are on the way up, you should delay your purchase until rates stabilise.

Annuity rates differ according to age and sex. The older you are the higher the payment. Indeed, until you reach 70, they are not really worthwhile. Women receive considerably lower rates than men of the same age because of their longer life expectancy.

Rates also vary substantially between companies and there is a big difference between what the best and worst companies will pay. You will need the help of a professional adviser in order to get the best terms.

Income on annuities is normally paid half-yearly, or quarterly in arrears but some insurers may also make monthly payments, though the overall annual return may then be somewhat lower.

The initial net return on annuities is usually high compared to other income producing investments because part of each payment is treated as a return of capital and is therefore untaxed. Only the interest portion is taxable. The capital element varies according to age and sex as the table on page 154 shows.

There are several different types of annuities including:

- Immediate annuities which provide regular level income payments until death. Married couples can purchase joint life and last survivor annuities which continue payments until both have died, and the initial return can be improved by agreeing to a reduction in payments, perhaps by one third, after the first death.
- Guaranteed annuities which continue to pay out for at least five or ten years, even if the annuitants die.
- Capital protected annuities which give a guarantee that the total gross payments will not be less than the purchase price of the annuity. If the annuitant dies before receiving the full amount, then a lump sum for the

Table 4

Capital element of the annual payment from an immediate annuity with a purchase price of £1000

Age	Male	Female
£	£	£
60	56.27	46.74
65	70.49	57.36
70	90.71	72.40
75	119.79	94.16
80	162.00	126.28

balance will be paid to his estate. Such guarantees have to be paid for, however, so the annual payments will be lower than under an annuity without guarantee.

- Increasing annuities which help to combat the main drawback of level payment annuities where the income may be rapidly eroded by inflation. They come in several forms. There are index linked annuities where payments increase in line with the RPI or escalating annuities where payments increase by a fixed percentage each year, say 3% or 5%. There are also with profits or unit linked annuities where payments depend on investment performance. The snag with these types of annuities is that your payments normally start lower than with a level annuity and can take sometime before they become higher. So they are advisable only for those in good health who are going to live to reap the benefits of the higher payments. It may be better to buy a smaller level annuity at first and use the remaining capital to buy further annuities when you are older and can get a higher annuity rate of which a larger part will be tax free.

A major disadvantage with annuities is that you lose control of your capital but there are income schemes involving annuities which attempt to get around this problem.

One is a scheme designed for a ten year term where an

immediate annuity is used both to provide an income for the investor and pay premiums on a with profits or unit linked endowment policy. At the end of the term the policy provides you with a return of capital. You cannot be absolutely certain of getting back your original investment at the end of the term, but there is a good chance that it may even be more.

Another scheme involves an investment being divided between an annuity and a unit trust or investment bond. This type of scheme is often constructed on a five-year timescale. The idea is that the unit trust or bond should grow sufficiently over the period to provide a return of capital and possibly provide some extra income as well. Investors will need to bear in mind, however, that this growth is not guaranteed.

Home income plans

The income schemes that have so far been discussed assume that you have spare capital to invest but the problem that confronts many older people is that most of their capital is tied up in their home. A way of unlocking this capital without having to move to a smaller property is through a home income plan.

The way most schemes work is that the homeowner raises a loan on his or her property from an insurance company or a building society and uses the money to buy an annuity. Part of the payments from the annuity cover the interest payments on the loan, net of basic rate tax relief, the remainder provides a useful boost to the homeowner's income. The capital is repayable from the proceeds of the sale of the property when the homeowner dies or moves.

How home income plans work

Example: Mrs Smith is a widow of 75 who lives in her own house worth £40,000. She receives the basic state pension, plus a small pension from her ex-employer and pays a small amount of tax. She obtains a loan of £30,000 through a home income plan. This provides extra income as follows:

Annuity purchase price £30,000		
Gross annuity	£3,705	
Less income tax on interest element	234	
Net annuity		3,471
DEDUCT		
Loan interest	2,475	
less tax relief at 25%	619	
Interest after tax relief		1,856
Net Annual Income		1,615
Net Monthly Income		134

Some home income schemes are based on a special low fixed mortgage rate with a lower than usual annuity rate to compensate, others give a more competitive annuity rate but charge the market rate of interest. The disadvantage of the latter is that if interest rates rise your income, which is fixed, will shrink. A fixed rate will give you more certainty.

Some schemes allow the interest to be rolled up and repaid at death along with the capital. An insurance policy may be offered to protect you against the possibility of your outstanding debt exceeding the value of your home.

Since they normally use annuities, home income schemes do not usually provide a worthwhile level of income unless you are over 70. Indeed 70 is the minimum age that companies will normally accept, and in the case of married couples a combined age of 150.

Loans of up to 80% of the value of the property are usually

Effect of age and sex on home income plan income

Single person – Net annual income

Age	Woman £	Man £
70	1,500	1,543
75	1,615	2,301
80	2,450	3,389

Couple – Net annual income

Age		
Both 75		1,027
Both 80		1,630

Source: Allied Dunbar, income based on loan of £30,000 assuming homeowner is basic rate taxpayer, figures as at January 1990

available, providing it is freehold or has a sufficient lease remaining. You may be allowed to take up to 10% of the loan as a cash sum, which could be particularly useful if there are repairs or improvements required to the property. A big advantage of these home income schemes is that it is often possible to go back to the lender for further loans as the value of the property appreciates. In this way, the income can be topped up.

Bear in mind that if you take out a home income scheme, your heirs will have to forego inheritance of that part of your property needed to repay the loan.

One type of home income plan which should be avoided if possible, is a home reversion scheme. This involves not mortgaging the house, but selling it outright. The planholder retains the right to reside in the house for life but as a result the price paid for the property will be below its market value. The apparent advantage of the scheme is that the homeowner can keep the whole of the annuity payment, since there will be no mortgage interest to pay. Major disadvantages, however, are that the homeowner and his or her heirs lose the benefit of any further increases in the value of the property, and that despite the fact that the property has been sold outright, the householder still has to maintain it at his or her own expense.

Summing up

- At retirement, remember you still have to plan for the long term as well as the short term.
- Take advantage of independent taxation by equalizing your income.
- Keep your tax position in mind when considering investments, particularly if you are in danger of falling into the age allowance trap.
- Consider taking part of your pension as a tax free lump sum.
- Try not to aim for maximum immediate income; look at schemes that offer the prospect of rising income
- Try to achieve a balanced income portfolio in order to protect your capital.
- If most of your capital is tied up in your home and your income is insufficient, consider a home income plan.

12 Financial advisers

The main purpose of this book has been to help you assess
your own financial goals and explore ways of achieving them.
But there are times when you may need professional help. So
who can you turn to for advice? Nowadays there are a wide
variety of financial advisers around. Some are better equipped
to give advice on certain matters than others, and it often
pays to seek two or three different opinions before making
your final decision.

In the past, many people felt uncertain about approaching
advisers because they felt they couldn't always be sure about
the adviser's level of expertise or honesty, or whether they
were getting only one company's view or a recommendation
that was influenced by the level of remuneration the adviser
was receiving.

Fortunately, because of the Financial Services Act, investors
can now feel more confident about the competence and financial
stability of the advisers they approach. Only those
intermediaries authorised as 'fit and proper' are allowed to
sell financial products.

Advisers also have to make it quite clear whether they are
tied to one company or are independent. Indeed, they have
to hand you a 'Buyer's Guide' which explains their status, at
the very start of your first meeting. If you buy an insurance
product, an independent financial adviser must give you a
statement showing how much commission he has recieved
as a percentage of your premiums. Company representatives
do not have to do so. But insurance companies do have to
provide information showing how their policy changes and

expenses (which includes the commission paid to representatives) affects policy payouts in the early years.

Independent financial advisers

Most advisers in this category are members of the Financial Intermediaries, Managers and Brokers Regulatory Association (FIMBRA). They are obliged to give you 'best advice' on the products in which they are authorised to deal. You can check they are authorised by contracting the Securities and Investment Board on 071–929 3652. Do not deal if the company is not fully authorised because you will not be eligible for compensation if something goes wrong.

In order to give you best advice an adviser will ask you for a considerable amount of personal information in order to establish your needs. He must then advise you on the best product to meet your needs from the whole market of products in which he deals. You are not obliged to provide information but if you tell the adviser what you want without taking his advice, this is called an 'execution only' deal and you won't be covered by compensation. The same applies if you buy through an advertisement in the press.

While some advisers are authorised to deal in certain products such as life insurance, pensions and unit trusts only, others can give on-going investment advice. They may offer discretionary unit trust management services, or their own broker managed investment bonds. Some offer a share dealing service. They may also help with the taxation aspects of your investments, such as recommending when 'bed-and-breakfasting' is necessary to take advantage of your capital gains tax allowance and providing you with the information you need for the taxman at the end of each tax year, in the form of schedules of transactions and dividend payments.

Some major players provide all round financial planning

services and can advise you on your life assurance, pensions and investment needs, taking into account taxation aspects as well, such as estate planning.

You do not normally have to pay directly for the advice that you get from independent financial advisers, unless you employ them to undertake discretionary management of your investments. Most of them derive their income from the commission payments they get from the insurance companies and unit trust groups whose products they sell.

The disadvantage of this system of remuneration, however, is that intermediaries are unlikely to recommend products on which they will earn no commission, such as National Savings products. It may also encourage some to recommend high commission products or, in the case of unit trusts, more switches than may be strictly necessary in order to generate more income for themselves. Moreover although you do not pay directly for the advice, you will foot the bill indirectly because the companies finance their commission payments through the charges they deduct from your investments.

Nevertheless, good advisers in this category have much to recommend them. They are independent. They have a good overview of the whole industry, they are normally happy to deal with smaller investors and know that their survival depends on giving a good service. Some now offer fee-based services which may cost you less in the long run.

Unless you are given a reliable recommendation, you can get the names of ten independent financial advisers in your area by ringing IFA Promotions Ltd on 081–200 3000.

In spite of the Financial Services Act, nobody can guarantee that some advisers will not go astray. Although there is a compensation fund in case an adviser is negligent in advising you or goes bust, it should not make you complacent. One way of ensuring temptation does not come an adviser's way is to make all your cheques out to the unit trust group, or insurance company concerned. Choosing an advisory service rather than discretionary management also means so that you can keep control over your money but you must then make the investment decisions.

If you have a complaint about an independent adviser contact the Investment Referee (see useful adresses section).

Company representatives

Many insurance companies have built up their own sales force to promote their products and services to the public. The large industrial insurers, such as the Prudential, the Pearl and the Co-operative, have used this method of selling and collecting premiums for many years and their representatives have a good public image. There are also some companies such as Equitable Life which rely on a salaried sales force because they do not pay commission to brokers.

During the 1970s when many new unit linked insurance companies were formed, the number of people selling life assurance and related services increased dramatically. This increasing competition resulted in the use of fairly aggressive sales techniques by some company representatives and there were a number of abuses. Nowadays, however, representatives have to be thoroughly trained, and in many cases they are licensed to sell specific products and are required to obey much tighter rules. Their company has to take full responsibility for their actions so if anything goes wrong, you will have resort to the company itself which, if it is keen to protect its reputation, will be anxious to put things right. The new financial services legislation lays down some stiff rules of conduct which all company representatives are obliged to follow and today's representatives operate in a very different world from that of the early 70s.

The advantage that representatives do have, or should, is a thorough knowledge of their own company's products. With increasing diversification by financial services groups these are likely to include not only life assurance and pension policies, but also unit trusts, personal equity plans, banking services and other products as well. Since representatives are now only allowed to promote the products of their own company, most companies have been anxious to ensure that their representatives have as full a portfolio of products as possible to offer.

Another advantage that a representative has is the technical back-up of his company. The world of financial services has grown increasingly more complex over recent years and the better companies now ensure that their representatives are supported by legal and technical services departments that can provide ready answers to the many technical problems that can arise.

The drawback of dealing with company representatives, however, is that they will only be able to advise you about and sell you the products of their own company, unlike an independent intermediary who should be able to recommend the best company in each product area. Some companies which deal through their own representatives offer competitive products which produce good results, and for this reason may also be recommended by intermediaries, so dealing through a representative is not necessarily a disadvantage. But, it will be up to you to establish the company's competitiveness, either by asking the representative to show you independent surveys of its results or by checking yourself in magazines such as *Planned Savings or Money Management*.

Nevertheless, no single company provides the best products in every area, and there may also be certain products which a company does not offer. For example, a wholly unit linked insurance company will not be able to provide with profits contracts and may not offer annuities. A with profits company may not offer unit trusts. So dealing with one company's representative alone could give you a one-sided view, though if the representative's company does not offer a particular product he will be able to direct you towards an independant advisor who might be able to help you.

If you have a complaint against a company representative, approach his or her company first. If you are not satisfied with the response, you can go to the Insurance Ombudsman Bureau or the Life Assurance and Unit Trust Regulatory Organisation (see useful adresses section).

Banks

Banks have traditionally been one of the most popular sources of financial advice because of their perceived trustworthiness and easy accessibility. Nowadays banks have specialist departments to provide advice on tax, insurance and investment matters. They also provide mortgages and many have established their own insurance and unit trust companies.

Most bank branches are now tied agents of their own insurance and investment companies but with separate companies within the banks acting as independent advisers for customers who request this service.

Of the main high street banks only the NatWest has decided to make itself fully independent.

The banks can arrange purchases and sales of shares and gilts on your behalf either through a specialist sharedealing arm or through a stockbroker. Dealing with a stockbroker in this way may work out more expensive than going direct as the bank will often make an additional charge on top of the stockbroker's own commission. If you want advice on which shares or gilts to buy this can also be arranged through the bank.

If you have a complaint against a bank, the body to go to will depend on the activity involved. If it is regarding investment advice see above. If it is to do with the banking side, contact the Banking Ombudsman (see useful adresses section).

Building societies

Until 1986, the range of services offered by the building societies was limited mainly to their traditional activities of deposit taking and mortgages. New legislation, however, has now given them the scope to expand their activities considerably if they wish.

Like the banks, building societies, under the Financial Services Act, have had to decide between selling just one company's insurance, pension products and unit trusts or advising customers on the full range of products available across the market. Most societies have decided to become tied agents of one particular insurance group. Customers should make sure to check the position of their society before seeking advice. Some societies can also provide independent advice through separate advisory arms, if so requested.

If you have a complaint about the investment advice a building society has given you see who to contact in sections above on company representatives and independent advisers. If it is a general complaint, go to the Building Societies Ombudsmen (see useful addresses section).

Accountants

Accountants are the best source of advice on personal and company tax matters. Providing they are authorised, they can also give advice on investment matters.

Some of the larger accountants have established specialist independent financial adviser departments to deal with this side of their business, others have teamed up with other independent intermediaries to offer a service. Those accountants who do not offer investment advice will be able to provide you with the names of financial advisers who can help you.

Unlike most advisers who derive their income from their commission earnings, accountants tend to work on a fee basis. Any commission they do earn will be declared and used to offset your fees.

If you have a complaint against an accountant go to your accountant's professional body (see useful adresses section).

Solicitors

For advice on legal matters, you should turn to a firm of solicitors. They may also be able to provide investment advice if authorised to do so. If not, they will be able to introduce you to advisers who can.

If you have a complaint about a solicitor contact the Law Society (see useful addresses section).

Stockbrokers

The role of stockbrokers has undergone various changes in recent years. In the past they dealt almost exclusively in stocks and shares on behalf of wealthier clients. But nowadays they are making themselves more accessible to smaller investors, and sometimes their services available through high street outlets such as department stores and building societies.

Although it is uneconomic for them to manage small portfolios of shares, they will provide share dealing services for small investors and will normally be prepared to give you advice on which shares and gilts to buy if you ask. Each stockbroking firm sets its own minimum level of commission, so if you are investing a small amount only it is a good idea to find out what competing firms charge in order to keep your costs down.

Some stockbrokers run their own unit trusts for use by smaller investors or will advise on which unit trusts to buy. They may be able to give advice on other types of investment also.

If you have a complaint about a stockbroker go to the Securities Association (see useful addresses section).

Other sources

Selling financial products is a lucrative business and a number of organisations such as retailers and motoring organisations are now recognising that it is possible for them to sell insurance and savings plans alongside their other goods and services. Once again, these companies are split between those which have linked with one financial institution and those which are acting as independent intermediaries. It is not always easy to distinguish because often the products are sold under the company's own label. Many of these organisations sell through the post. It is best to avoid buying financial products through the post, however, since they are designed for a mass market rather than to meet your requirements, and in any case you may well find you can get more competitive terms elsewhere.

Making the final decision

Getting the advice of professionals can be very useful but in the end the decision on which course of action to take will be yours. After reading this book you should be better equipped to make the right decisions.

Useful addresses

Advisers

Financial Intermediaries, Managers and Brokers Regulatory
   Association (FIMBRA)
Hertsmere House, Marsh Wall
London E14 9RW

British Insurance and Investment Brokers Association
   (BIIBA)
14 Bevis Marks
London EC3A 7NT

Insurance Brokers Registration Council
15 St Helens Place
London EC3A 6DS

Association of Certified Accountants
29 Lincoln's Inn Fields
London WC2A 3EE

Institute of Chartered Accountants in England and Wales
Chartered Accountants Hall
Moorgate Place
London EC2P 2BJ

Institute of Chartered Accountants of Scotland
27 Queen Street
Edinburgh EH2 1LA

Incorporated Society of Valuers and Auctioneers
3 Cadogan Gate
London SW1X 0AS

Law Society
Ipsley Court
Berrington Close
Redditch
Worcestershire B98 0TD

Law Society of Scotland
Law Society's Hall
26 Drumsheugh Gardens
Edinburgh EH3 7YR

Institute of Public Loss Assessors
14 Red Lion Street
Chesham Bucks

Citizens' Advice Bureau
(see telephone directory
for your local branch)

Complaints

Parliamentary Commissioner and Health Service
   Commissioner
Church House
Great Smith Street
London SW1P 3BW

Insurance Ombudsman Bureau
31 Southampton Row
London WC1B 5HJ

Personal Insurance Arbitration Service
75 Cannon Street
London EC4N 5BH

Office of the Banking Ombudsman
Citadel House
5/11 Fetter Lane
London EC4A 1BR

Building Society Ombudsman
Grosvenor Gardens House
35 – 37 Grosvenor Gardens
London SW1X 7AW

Solicitors Complaints Bureau
Portland House
Stag Place
London SW1

Securities Association
The Stock Exchange
Old Broad Street
London EC2N 1HP

The Investment Referee
6 Frederick's Place
London EC2R 8BT

Unit Trust Ombudsman
31 Southampton Row
London WC1B 5HJ

Insurance

Association of British Insurers
Aldermary House
Queen Street
London EC4N 1TT

Investment

The Securities Association
The Stock Exchange
London EC2N 1HP

Unit Trust Association
65 Kingsway
London WC2B 6TD

Association of Investment Trust Companies
6th Floor
Park House
16 Finsbury Circus
London EC2M 7JJ

Securities and Investment Board (SIB)
3 Royal Exchange Buildings
London EC3V 3NL

Life Assurance and Unit Trust
Regulatory Organisation (LAUTRO)
Centre Point
103 New Oxford Street
London WC1A 1QH

Investment Management Regulatory Organisation (IMRO)
Centre Point
103 New Oxford Street
London WC1A 1PT

Pensions and retirement

Age Concern
Bernard Sunley House
60 Pitcairn Road
Mitcham Surrey
CR4 3LL

National Association of Pension Funds (NAPF)
12–18 Grosvenor Gardens
London SW1W 0DH

Occupational Pensions Advisory Service
8a Bloomsbury Square
London WC1

Banks, building societies, and national savings

Banking Information Service
10 Lombard Street
London EC3V 9AR

Building Societies Association
3 Savile Row
London W1X 1AF

Department of National Savings
Charles House
375 Kensington High Street
London W14 8SD

Index

Other titles in the Allied Dunbar Library